Arab Evangelicals in Israel

ARAB EVANGELICALS IN ISRAEL

Azar Ajaj,
Duane Alexander Miller,
and Philip Sumpter

PICKWICK *Publications* • Eugene, Oregon

ARAB EVANGELICALS IN ISRAEL

Pickwick Publications
An Imprint of Wipf and Stock Publishers
199 W. 8th Ave., Suite 3
Eugene, OR 97401

www.wipfandstock.com

PAPERBACK ISBN: 978-1-4982-7951-2
HARDCOVER ISBN: 978-1-4982-7953-6
EBOOK ISBN: 978-1-4982-7952-9

Cataloguing-in-Publication data:

Names: Ajaj, Azar.

Title: Arab evangelicals in Israel / Azar Ajaj, Duane Alexander Miller, and Philip Sumpter.

Description: Eugene, OR: Pickwick Publications, 2016 | Includes bibliographical references.

Identifiers: ISBN 978-1-4982-7951-2 (paperback) | ISBN 978-1-4982-7953-6 (hardcover) | ISBN 978-1-4982-7952-9 (ebook)

Subjects: LCSH: Palestinian Arabs—Israel—Religion. | Christians—Israel. | Palestine—Religion. | Miller, Duance Alexander. | Sumpter, Philip. | Title.

Classification: BS1160 A91 2016 (paperback) | BS1160 (ebook)

Manufactured in the U.S.A. 07/08/16

This book is dedicated to the body of Christ in Israel-Palestine,
both Jewish and Arab.

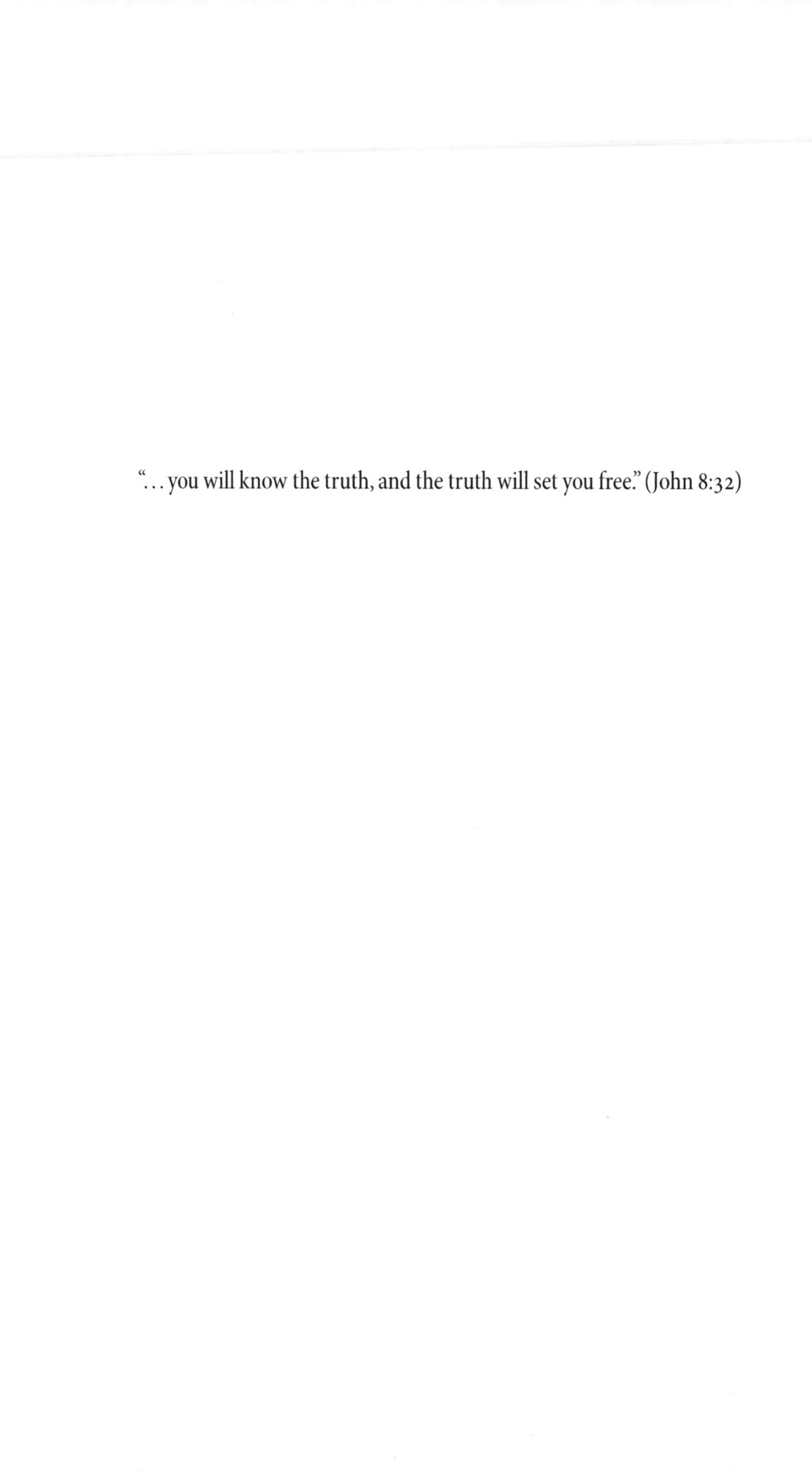

"... you will know the truth, and the truth will set you free." (John 8:32)

Contents

Introduction

THIS COLLECTION OF ESSAYS has been put together by three members of the faculty at Nazareth Evangelical Theological Seminary (NETS) in Nazareth, Israel, the predecessor of what is now Nazareth Evangelical College (NEC). The projected was undertaken as part of that institution's mission to understand, minister to, and communicate to a broader audience the concerns, challenges, and hopes of indigenous Arab Christianity in Israel, in particular evangelical Christianity.

The subjects of each chapter are introductory in nature, for they serve to acquaint the reader with different aspects of Arab evangelical life in Israel (and to a lesser degree in the West Bank). The first chapter is the broadest in scope: it opens with a historical sketch of the experience of the indigenous church in the region from the time of Christ until 2013. This story is not told out of antiquarian interest but as vital background for understanding the present, which is the subject of the second half of the chapter. Repeated patterns are pointed out and contemporary complexities explicated in light of past developments. A key focus of this chapter is on the church as an actor that effects change rather than being a passive subject of historical forces greater than it. Of particular interest are the insights we have garnered from living and ministering among Arabs in Israel and from field work conducted in the West Bank.

Having set the broader historical, political, and economic context, the following chapters focus on specific details of evangelical experience. Chapter 2 introduces the first attempt in the Middle East to unite all evangelical denominations into a single body in a bid to gain recognition from the government as a single denomination, namely the Convention of Evangelical Christians in Israel (CECI). Although this indigenous Arab initiative has not yet achieved its initial goal of state recognition, its cross-denominational focus and communal activities have created a number of other benefits along the way, along with some unexpected challenges.

This broad denominational focus is narrowed down in chapter 3, which takes a look at the largest and oldest evangelical Free Church denomination in Israel, the Baptists. After a brief sketch of the history of this denomination, the chapter inquires into the self-identity of Baptist church leaders within the context of the confusing and conflicting array of options within the nation. It appears that a defining mark of Baptist identity among the options "Palestinian," "Israeli," "Arab," "Communist," "Christian," etc., is their commitment to the "evangel," the "gospel of Jesus Christ"; this is seen to be primary factor which overrides all other commitments.

Chapter 4 turns to a project initiated by the indigenous Arab Association of Baptist Churches in Israel (ABCI) to provide theological education for the leaders of the broader Arab evangelical community. The initial result was Nazareth Evangelical Theological Seminary (NETS), an institution set up by the Scottish missionaries Bryson and May Arthur. This institution recently merged with the very small Galilee Bible College to become an entirely indigenous operation under the new name Nazareth Evangelical College (NEC). It is the only institution of its kind in the country.

Chapter 5 returns to look at an important and complex relationship in which many Arab Israeli evangelicals are involved, namely their relationship with that other significant evangelical community within Israel, the Messianic Jews. Through interviews with all local Arab leaders, the frustrations and hopes of the Arab side of the dialogue are presented and analyzed, along with suggestions for how this relationship could be developed in the future.

The final substantive chapter of this book (chapter 6) looks at the struggles, hopes, and fears of another "evangelical" community that is usually hidden from view, namely that of Muslim converts to Christianity in Israel, the West Bank, and the Middle East in general. This community is not necessarily "evangelical," either in terms of the source of the conversion or in terms of the Christian community to which the convert seeks to belong, but due to the dangerous status of Muslim "apostates" in Muslim dominant areas and a history of non- (indeed anti-)evangelism among traditional churches, it is usually the evangelical strain of Christianity which either reaches out to these Muslims or accepts them among their ranks.

The final chapter offers as exhaustive a bibliography as possible of everything published on "Arabophone Christianity" in Israel and Palestine until the year 2013.

A few words should be said about the contributors to this volume: Azar Ajaj is an indigenous Arab Israeli and first generation convert to evangelical Christianity (his background is Greek Catholic). As a Baptist pastor, Director of Public Relations, and lecturer at what has now become Nazareth Evangelical College (NEC), he has deep connections with the evangelical Arab community and a thorough knowledge of its history and current challenges. He is currently writing a PhD on the history of the Baptist church in the Holy Land.

Duane Alexander Miller has been on the faculty of NETS for five years and has seven years' experience living in the Middle East among Arabs. His knowledge of the language, history, and culture of the region has been further deepened through field-work based doctoral work on Muslim converts to Christianity. Together with Philip Sumpter he contributed in 2013 to the Berkley Center's "Christianity and Freedom" project by providing field work on attitudes of Arab Christians in the West Bank to religious, political, and economic freedom.

Philip Sumpter has a PhD in Old Testament and has served for a year at NETS as tutor, lecturer, and research assistant. In 2013 he participated with D. Alex Miller on field research into Christianity in the West Bank for the Berkley Center's "Christianity and Freedom" project.

CHAPTER 1

Christian Agency in Israel-Palestine

Historical Background and Contemporary Observations

by Philip Sumpter

1. INTRODUCTION

In order to contextualize the following chapters on evangelical Christianity among Arabs in Israel, this chapter has a two-fold focus. In §2 "Historical Overview" is provides the historical context of Christianity in the Holy Land in general, starting with the earliest movement two thousand years ago leading up to the contemporary situation in 2013. One may ask whether such a broad view is necessary for a book with such a particular focus as ours, but as the following will demonstrate, things change very slowly in the Middle East and for even such a fast-evolving nation as the State of Israel the contemporary scene not only bears many analogies with the past but also can only be understood in light of it. This historical overview, then, provides the framework for § 3 "Christian Agency in Contemporary Israel-Palestine." In this section the focus is on Arab Christians in the contemporary world of Israel-Palestine, actors who are not only the object of historical forces but also intentional agents of change who are seeking to mold a future for themselves. Observations in this section are based both on secondary literature but more importantly on our experience of living and researching in the region. The connections between the historical overview and contemporary analysis will be made clear by means of cross-references as the chapter unfolds.

2. HISTORICAL OVERVIEW

2.1. Jewish and Pagan Beginnings

Israel-Palestine is often called the "cradle of Christianity," and the metaphor is fitting in that its Lord was born there and had his horizons shaped by a nation—the people of Israel—that claimed a special relation to it. However, it is also the case—and this will prove decisive for all that follows—that the major part of that nation rejected his mission, which found more fruitful soil in the hearts of the pagan Gentiles. The major tenets and institutions of the Christians faith were formed outside of the land in Rome, Alexandria, and Constantinople.[1] Indeed, the gradual Christianization of the land itself came about through the activities of monks from the neighboring regions such as Antioch and Egypt, and received its greatest impetus through the decision of the Byzantine emperor Theodosius the Great (379–395) to make Orthodox Christianity the religion of the state. For the rest of the history of the region until this very day, the major vehicle and institutional representation of Christian faith would be in hands of a church—in time the Greek Orthodox Church—that understood itself to be intimately connected to the Hellenic culture and language of Byzantium. As the state religion it was to impose itself on other forms of Christianity that differed in language (such as Syriac) and nuances of doctrine (in particular Monophysitism).

Despite its relatively limited contribution to the ongoing life of the church in terms of producing theological revolutions, what one might call "secondary discourse," the geography itself has always retained a special place in the heart of Christendom because of its role within the divine economy and thus its capacity to provide what might be called "primary discourse," a revelation and communication of the kingdom of God.[2] As such, to this day global Christianity has retained a fascination with the land, bestowing it with religious institutions, hospices, and hostels to cater for the needs of its pilgrims and their thirst for spiritual immediacy. Colbi

1. Saul Colbi, *A Short History.*
2. Jerome (347–420) called the land itself the "fifth gospel."

notes that the Crusader kingdom of Jerusalem contained Greek Orthodox, Syrian Jacobites, Maronites, Ethiopians, Copts, Armenians, Nestorians and Georgians.[3] A similar diversity can be found in Jerusalem today.[4]

2.2. Muslim Conquest

The notorious Byzantine oppression of those outside of its religious system which was later continued by the Crusaders has also had consequences to this day: the Jewish State of Israel still harbors enmity against the Church due to years of anti-Jewish persecution,[5] whereas Palestinian Christian theologians often choose to identify themselves as the descendants of the original indigenous church that had been oppressed by Western Crusader foreigners as part of their bid to create solidarity with the Muslim Arab majority (see §3.2). The discontent created fertile ground for the seventh century invasions of the Muslim *mujahidin*, as many Syriac Christians felt that the new Arab order would provide them with more freedom than their Greek overlords. There are indications that the situation improved at first, but over time the condition of *dhimmitude*, for Muslims the legal requirement for their continued existence, did not prove to be as liberating as hoped. A large measure of freedom was granted in terms of inner-community religious practices (though the evangelism that had created the churches in the first place was now forbidden on pain of death [see chapter 6 of this book]) as well as matters of personal status. However, they were subjected to laws such as the *djiziah* (a special tax) designed to humiliate them, limit their influence, and sap their energy. Over time the *dar al-harb* ("the house of war," i.e., those outside Islam) gradually receded while the *dar al-islam* ("the house of peace," i.e., those inside Islam) grew.

The spiritual practice of pilgrimage was not initially interrupted by the Muslim invasion, and so the churches of Europe did not provide an immediate political response. With succeeding Muslim dynasties, however, conditions worsened for local Christians. New churches could not be built, the cross could not be displayed, public liturgy was circumscribed, distinctive signs had to be worn, horses could not be rode upon, tapers could

3. Colbi, *A Short History*, 23.

4. See Tsimhoni, *Christian Communities*.

5. See, for example, the recent report on Church-State relations in Israel by Ramon, *Christians and Christianity*. A detailed English-language synopsis can be found online at this address, http://www.jiis.org.il/.upload/christianspdf-eng%20abstract.pdf.

not be kindled, church bells could not be rung.[6] Things did improve with foreign intervention in the form of negotiations with the Muslim rulers. For example, Charlemagne (742/747/748–814), a useful political ally, received the right of "protectorate" over the Holy Places, the Holy Land, and its Christian inhabitants, whose lot then improved with the investments made in monasteries, libraries and hospices for pilgrims. Even before the great church schism between East and West (1054), however, such political maneuverings created tensions between these two halves of Chalcedonian Christendom. The Byzantine emperors still laid claim to the land and so they too gradually re-increased their sphere of influence by means of both small-scale military campaigns for parts of the land as well as negotiations for the right to be regarded as protectors of the holy places.

As shall be seen in §3 below, foreign pilgrimage, foreign advocacy, inner-Christian rivalry, and the division of the population into partially autonomous religious communities continue to be defining features of the Christian landscape in contemporary Israel-Palestine.

2.3. Christian Response

The invasion of the Holy Land by the Seljuk Turks led to the massacre of its Christian inhabitants, desecration of their holy places, and inhibited the ability of pilgrims to approach them. This sent off alarm bells in Christian Europe. Although the ensuing Crusades had multiple causes, it is arguable that the primary factor was this violation of their religious "right" along with the cries of the indigenous Christians for outside intervention. The Crusaders introduced the culture and theology of Europe—the French and Germanic elements were particularly prominent—but the new kingdoms created political innovations of their own. For example, new forms of administration gave much power to the laity instead of the clergy. The lot of the local Christians, however, did not improve as much as hoped. The Greeks were offended by the installation of a Latin patriarch in Jerusalem to replace their own and non-Latin Christians were subjected to further discrimination, so much so that those regions with a high population of "Easterners" ended up welcoming the re-entry of Islam.[7] The final victorious battle at the Horns of Hattin in 1187 marked the beginning of Muslim

6. Colbi, *A Short History*, 17–18.

7. Ibid., 23.

hegemony in the region—despite repeated attempts by Christendom to regain it— until the entry of the British in 1917.

2.4. Muslim Reconquest

In the intervening 700 years, the Holy Land became a backwater of larger Muslim empires. Under the Mamlukes the number of pilgrims dwindled due to the imposition of burdensome tolls while the life of Christians became more and more difficult and dangerous.[8] Muslims considered themselves legal owners of Christian shrines by right of conquest, the rights to which they could determine at will. This fact has consequences for today, because it meant that it was impossible for the various Christian denominations to find satisfactory legal solutions to their competing claims of ownership.[9] Concessions granted were determined by either bribery or political exigency—significant given the international connections of the churches.[10] This power became a useful tool in gaining leverage with both local Christians and international powers, a technique still used by the Israeli government today (see §§2.6.1; 2.7.1).

Under the Ottomans the Greek Orthodox managed to gain the upper hand in the struggle to embody Christendom in the Holy Land. As the major church in Ottoman domains (Constantinople; Alexandria; Antioch; Jerusalem), this church was recognized as the sole official *millet*, the Turkish form of a *dhimmi*, within the empire. This accorded this particular denomination much power, as religious communities were also national entities with their own law courts and representatives to the government.[11] Although in time other denominations came to be recognized, the effect on Israel-Palestine of this initial hegemony was that smaller sects such as the Nestorians and Jacobites, once so populous in the region, were gradually absorbed into Orthodoxy.[12]

8. According to Colbi, under the Mamelukes the Christians were almost taxed out of existence (ibid., 36).

9. See O'Mahony, "Palestinian Christians," 16.

10. Colbi, *A Short History*, 35

11. Farah claims that the *dhimmi/millet* system actually contributed to the hegemony of the clergy over their faithful in civil as well as spiritual matters, as they were representatives of this sphere to the Islamic government, from which Christians were otherwise excluded. See Farah, *Christian Presence*, 136.

12. Tsimhoni, *Christian Communities*, xv.

In time, a further concentration of power took place which would have an abiding effect on indigenous Palestinian Christianity: the concentration of ecclesial power in the hands of *ethnic* Greeks alone (this process of "Hellenization" started under Patriarch German [1534–1579]). Today, Greek Orthodox Palestinians still talk of the "Greek occupation" of their church (see §3.2).

Until the end of Turkish rule, the remainder of the history of Christianity in the Holy Land was, as Colbi puts it, "little more than a chronicle of quarrel after quarrel between Latins and Orthodox for possession of the Holy Places."[13] Both sides made gains and losses. Primarily under the influence of France the Latins gained the upper hand in the form of the Franciscans, at one point the Russians set down roots, much to the chagrin of their Greek brothers in the Orthodox faith (the Russian connection was a factor in acquainting many Palestinian Christians with communism, a major source of Christian Arab Israeli identification to this day [see §2.7.1]), but ultimately the Orthodox were able to regain a position of prominence. This prominence was then guaranteed, seemingly in perpetuity, in 1757 when the *de facto* conditions on the ground were finally fixed in law and made unalterable. This marks the beginning of the famous *Status Quo*, an agreement that stayed in force until Israel strategically decided to omit it from its obligations to the holy places following its annexation of East Jerusalem in 1967 (see §2.7.1).

The lot of Christians during what Atallah Mansour calls "the long dark night of the Ottoman empire" remained unchanged.[14] Though Western powers sought to improve their situation by influencing the Turkish government during the nineteenth century, only minimal progress was made (both patriarchates of Jerusalem, the Greek and the recently reinstalled Latin one, strongly resisted attempts to empower the laity).[15] It is during this period that Christians were to develop two strategies for achieving freedom that have continued under various modifications to this day: emigration and advocacy for a secular form of government, in particular

13. Colbi, *A Short History*, 38. O'Mahony traces this development back to the Mamluke period. Since that time, "the history of Jeruslam is primarily a history of continual change of status, of rights of ownership and of position among the various Christian communities in the Holy Places. Although it should be noted that the majority of the Christian inhabitants of Jerusalem were Eastern or Oriental Christians, whatever happened in the Holy Places" ("Palestinian Christians," 15–16).

14. Mansour, *Narrow Gate Churches*. This phrase is repeated like a refrain in his book.

15. O'Mahony, "Palestinian Christians," 20.

one based on national rather than religious affiliation (see §4; we will see that in recent years the second option has started to crumble). The latter development was inspired by parallel developments in Europe at the time. Christians in particular had access to these ideas because of the activities of Western missionaries enflamed by the religious revivals at home. These missionaries not only brought new forms of ecclesial existence to the East—the Protestant churches with their emphasis on literacy, education, and lay participation marked a particular break (see chapter 3 in this book)—they also brought schools in which to educate a new generation in the ways of the West.[16] To this day, Christian Palestinians are characterized by their high education levels, political involvement, and ability to represent the cause of their people to the outside world (see §3.2). The missionary activity of the Protestant and Catholic churches also decidedly fragmented the Palestinian church, as the vast majority of their members were taken from the Orthodox. Today, the State of Israel recognizes the following Christian *'edot moqorot* ("recognized communities," the Israeli version of the *millet*) Greek Orthodox, Roman Catholic, Greek Catholic, Armenian Catholic, Chaldean Catholic, Syrian Catholic, Maronite, Armenian Orthodox, Syrian Orthodox, and Anglican.

2.5. The British Mandatory Period (1917–1947)

Following the dissolution of the Ottoman Empire, the League of Nations allotted the mandate for Palestine to Britain. British concern for the welfare of the mandate's inhabitants, regardless of religion (Christians did not receive special treatment), led to a marked improvement in the quality of life for all, even stemming the flow of Christian emigration. They adopted the *millet* system with the important innovation that there was no state religion, with the result that for the first time Muslims themselves were to become a *millet*, on equal footing alongside the Christians, Jews, and others.

At the turn of the last century, the world was as secular as it ever has been. The "sleeping dragon of Islam" had not yet been awakened so that the development of new communal and thus political identities based on factors other than religion gained in credibility in Muslim and Christian circles. In the Middle East "Arabism" grew in popularity, an ideology which

16. The connection between being Protestant, educated, and politically aware is proudly pointed out by the Arab Israeli Anglican clergyman and Palestinian nationalist Abu El-Assal in *Caught in Between*.

claims that one's "nationality" is more socially and politically significant than one's religion, which was now to be seen as a private affair. Christians were the driving force behind this movement and the attraction is clear: as Christians in a society organized according to Islamic law they would always be second class citizens. If one's "Arabness" is the principle factor, then they could finally be accepted as full and equal participants within the broader community. One consequence of this development in British Palestine was that it was the Christians who first became aware of what they perceived as the Zionist threat and it was they who organized resistance to it. This led the first Zionist leaders to conclude that antipathy towards Jewish immigrants came mostly from Christian rather than Muslim circles.[17]

As a foretaste of later experiences, however, even at this early stage Arab nationalism in Palestine never managed to become fully secular. Over time, the Muslim majority involved in the movement came to stress the centrality of Islam for a future Palestinian entity. Christian Arab nationalist responses had to accommodate this all-pervasive facet of Middle Eastern culture, affirming the value of the religion as a unifying factor, as the guarantor of good manners, wise regulations, wisdom, all the while asserting that as Christians they had an equally valuable contribution to make to the Islamized Arab project. As we shall see (§3.2), this tension in freely choosing to remain loyal to a Muslim majority whose religion subordinated them has continued to this day. It is revealing that as early as the turn of the last century Kahlil al-Sakakini, a prominent Palestinian Christian Arab nationalist thinker, could write the following words to his son in America: "as long as I am not a Moslem I am nought. . . . I only pray . . . that you will not return to this country until it has changed, and when a man will be estimated by what he achieves and not according to how he preserves these outworn customs . . ."[18]

2.6. Jewish and Jordanian Rule: 1948–1967

The 1948 war between the newly proclaimed Jewish state and its Arab neighbors resulted in the partition of the land into three regions: Jordan annexed the West Bank, along with East Jerusalem, Egypt occupied Gaza, and Israel gained control of the rest (the Golan Heights remained in Syrian hands until the Six Day War in 1967). The impact was traumatic for all the

17. O'Mahony, "Palestinian Christians," 47.

18. Ibid., 52.

local Arabs, regardless of religion. Within the boundaries of the State of Israel, many fled their homes to the neighboring countries, never to return, others were forcibly driven out by Israeli forces and either sent abroad or relocated within Israel, with the original property either being destroyed or turned over to the new government (much of which was given to new Jewish immigrants). Recounting these experiences for a Western audience has been one of the strategies used by Palestinian Christians to further the cause of the Palestinian people as a whole. One successful example is the Greek Catholic bishop Elias Chacour's highly "poeticized" account of the destruction of his rural village in the Galilee (Bir'am) and his attempt to rebuild the Arab community in Israel.[19] Importantly, the Christian villages were entirely peaceful, not participating in the conflict.[20]

2.6.1. Christians in Israel

Following the ceasefire, those Arab citizens who remained within the boundaries of the new Jewish state along with those who could return on the basis of the Reunion of Families Scheme[21] were subject to martial law until 1966. This involved travel permits, curfews, and administrative detentions. They were also granted Israeli citizenship, which entitled them to vote for the Israeli Knesset, some of whose members have been Arabs. Following the lifting of martial law Arab citizens were granted—so Israel claims—the same rights as Jewish citizens under law. The degree to which this is in fact true, either in theory or in practice, is debated. Many Palestinian-Israelis, both in conversation and in print,[22] claim that they are "second class citizens," pointing out discrimination on various levels, such as lack of investment in Arab areas, unfair continued expropriation of their land, projects to "Judaize" regions with a high Arab population, difficulties in

19. Chacour, *Blood Brothers*. We say that his account is "poeticized" as parts of it are actually fictional, even if presented as fact. For example, an Arab journalist of Chacour's generation who lived in the village Chacour moved to has said that his description of villagers accepting Jewish soldiers as guests in their homes is an "outright lie." Other examples are Naim Ateek's biographical sketch of his deportation from Beisan in *Justice and Only Justice* and Atallah Mansour's memories in *Narrow Gate Churches*.

20. For details, see Morris, *Refugee Problem*.

21. Abu El-Assal reports the difficulties his family experienced with this scheme in *Caught in Between*.

22. See, for example, Farah, *Christian Presence*, 79. In our opinion, Attallah Mansour's *Narrow Gate Churches* provides a more balanced picture of the Arab situation in Israel.

getting work and housing, etc. One significant problem is their inability to *identify* with the new Jewish state. For example, the national hymn is written from the perspective of a Diaspora Jew yearning to immigrate to Zion, something an Arab cannot sing no matter how much he or she may wish to identify with the State. Once again they are outsiders in a system that, although it is able to provide them with more economic opportunities and political freedoms than other countries in the Middle East, has not created the ideological space to accept them as an intricate part of the nation.[23] It is beyond the scope of this chapter, however, to analyze the legal status of Israel's Arabs *as Arabs*. Our focus is on the status of Israel's Christians *as Christians*, the vast majority of whom are in fact Arab.

From the outset, the new Jewish state saw itself as a liberal, secular democracy that guaranteed the social and political equality of all its citizens, without distinction of religion, race or sex. In light of the situation of conflict as well as Israel's own interests in securing and furthering its Jewishness, however, relations with its Christians—whether the still largely foreign-dominated church hierarchy or the indigenous Arab laity—cannot be described as particularly altruistic.[24] Both Dumper and Ramon describe how the state's dealings with the churches were influenced by a number of conflicting spheres of interest as well as historical baggage. In terms of memories from the past, the long history of Christian persecution of Jews as well as the Arab nationalist aspirations of many Christians (see §§2.7.2; 3) did not generate trust or sympathy on the part of their new overlords.[25] On the other hand, Israel desired get its hands on the extensive lands that were still church property while retaining legitimacy in the eyes of the powerful international Christian community. The fragmented nature of the local churches enable it to negotiate with each denomination on an individual basis, their policies varying depending on the power of the states or international entities that stood behind them, the degree of their "Arabization," the size of the community in Israel, and the extent of the denomination's missionary activity.[26] Denominations lacking the status of *'edah moqeret* (the former *millet*) such as the Anglicans (who only received recognition

23. This is conceded by the Zionist thinker Avrum Ehrlich in "Attitudes of Arab Christianity." He goes on to make some tentative suggestions about now Jewish theology could remedy the situation.

24. Dumper, "Faith and Statecraft," 56–81; Ramon, "Christians and Christianity."

25. Tsimhoni, *Christian Communities*; Ramon, "Christians and Christianity," iv.

26. Ramon, "Christians and Christianity," vi.

at a later date) had the hardest time; the relative weakness of Greece meant that the Orthodox did not receive preferential treatment, despite the larger size of the church. The international leverage of the Vatican, however, did lead to the meeting of many of the Latin Church's needs, this despite the fact that until the Oslo Agreement the Vatican was one of the staunchest critics of Israeli policy.[27]

The concerns that needed to be met were the return of property or reparations for its damage during the war, the granting of tax and custom exemptions long enjoyed under the Ottomans, the granting of circumscribed autonomy to churches, the permitting of the churches in Israeli West Jerusalem to maintain contact with their centers in Jordanian East Jerusalem, and the provision of visas.[28] On none of these issues did Israel codify laws or establish obligatory norms. This enabled it to use the "carrot and stick" approach, granting concessions if and when it pleased, depending on the pliability of its beneficiaries (note the similarities to the Muslim approach in §2.4). To add to the confusion, to this day there is no single state department with a coherent policy for handling Christian affairs. Many positions of influence belong to the religious-nationalist parties, who are more concerned than their liberal counterparts to quell the thriving of Christianity in the country.[29]

2.6.2. *Christians in Jordan*

The Hashemite Kingdom of Jordan's annexation of the West Bank and East Jerusalem placed its new citizens under a moderate Muslim Arab regime influenced by the sentiments of Arab nationalism.[30] As such, although Islam was the official religion, the constitution guaranteed freedom and equality before the law for all citizens regardless of religion and race. The constitution also recognized the right of Christian and foreign communities to maintain their own educational institutions, provided these were supervised by the government.[31] However, Dumper argues that Jordan was

27. See, for example, the brief but insightful treatment in Dumper, "Faith and Statecraft."

28. In addition to Dumper and Ramon, see Mack, "Christian Palestinian Communities," 292–95.

29. See Dumper and Ramon.

30. O'Mahony, "Palestinian Christians," 55.

31. Tsimhoni, *Christian Communities*, 1.

also at pains to establish its Muslim credentials as guardian of Jerusalem, the third holiest site in Islam. As such, it took measures to limit the progress that Christians had been making since the mandate period.[32] In Jerusalem, strict limitations were placed upon the opportunities for the churches to purchase land and develop property. In 1953 a law was passed restricting the purchase of property "by religious and charitable organizations, which constitute branches of a foreign body." Letters of protest and delegations were sent by the Christians communities protesting the law, and even the Pope raised the issue when visited by the king in 1953. The restrictions were ameliorated to a degree, but pressure by Muslim circles led the government to prohibit Christian institutions from buying properties in the neighborhood of the holy places. Later this included property within the walls of Old Jerusalem.[33] Furthermore, "since Christian run schools were more affluent, better equipped and staffed and attracted large numbers of Muslim students, greater supervision and some restrictions were introduced. A ceiling for the number of students was set and amendments made to the curricula which included the teaching of the Qur'an."[34]

The war of 1948 was particularly catastrophic for Jerusalem's indigenous Christian population. Most lived in the western part, which fell to Israel. They first fled to the Eastern part, losing everything they had, and then—given their unwillingness as educated members of the middle class to accept the dire economic conditions of that part of the city—moved on to the West Bank, Jordan, Lebanon, and the West.[35] According to one estimate, between 1948 and 1967 the Christian population of East Jerusalem dropped from 38 percent of the total population to just 15 percent.[36]

2.7. Jewish and the Beginnings of Palestinian Rule: 1967–2013.

2.7.1. Christians in Israel

A year after Israel lifted martial law from its Arab citizens it successfully gained control of the Golan Heights (under Syria), the West Bank and East

32. Dumper, "Faith and Statecraft," 60.

33. Tsimhoni, *Christian Communities*, 3.

34. Dumper, "Faith and Statecraft," 60–61. For more details see Tsimhoni, *Christian Communities*.

35. Tsimhoni, *Christian Communities*, 19.

36. Prittie, *Whose Jerusalem*, cited in Dumper, "Faith and Statecraft," 59–60.

Jerusalem (under Jordan), and Gaza/Sinai (under Egypt). The Sinai Peninsula was eventually returned to Egypt in the seventies after the two signed a peace treaty, the Golan Heights and East Jerusalem were annexed, and the West Bank remained under Israeli military occupation.

Israel's annexation of East Jerusalem brought some of the holiest shrines of Christendom under its power. In accordance with the Geneva Convention, in 1967 the government passed the Protection of Holy Places Law, which assured freedom of access to and protection of the holy places. In line with the aforementioned "carrot and stick" strategy of relating to the individual churches, Israel did not commit itself to maintaining the *Status Quo* (see §2.4).[37] In practice however, it has tended not to interfere in internal church matters. A prominent exception was its decision to resolve a dispute between the Coptic and Ethiopian Churches concerning ownership of a portion of the Church of the Holy Sepulcher (Deir al-Sultan), a move motivated by its strategic relationship with Ethiopia.[38]

Israel's treatment of the established churches has, by and large, stood them in good stead. Property damaged or confiscated during Israel's various wars has either been repaired or returned and financial reparations have been forthcoming. Furthermore, the restrictions that had been placed on the churches and church bodies under Jordanian rule have been removed.[39] Israel's treatment of the church hierarchy, however, has not been matched by preferential treatment of its Arab Christians—either in Israel or the disputed territories.[40] Instead, both have been seen as "Arabs," for which their religious identity is insignificant. The result was an increased sense of national solidarity between Christians and Muslims, as both shared the same fate. This has not only been a matter of policy, as Ramon and Tsimhoni point out (they also argue it was a strategic mistake), it also accords with Palestinian experience. As one of Bowman's interviewees from the West Bank put it in 1990, "We forget our religion; we forget our political groups.

37. Dumper, "Faith and Statecraft," 64.

38. For details, see Tsimhoni, *Christian Communities.*

39. Ramon, "Christians and Christianity," viii.

40. Ibid., vii; Tsimhoni, *Christian Communities*, 175. After analysing Israeli policy concerning the route of the West Bank separation barrier, Amnon Ramon concludes that "the Israeli willingness to ease restrictions on Palestinian Christians is weaker than the desire to accommodate foreign bodies which have the backing of the Vatican or other international entities" ("Christian Institutions," 135).

The bullets do not differentiate between Christian and Muslim, PLO, DFLP, etc."[41]

A brief statement should be made here about Christian-Muslim relations in Israel, given the prominence this theme will have below (§3). The historically relatively peaceful co-existence between Arab Christians and Muslims is often pointed out by scholars and locals alike.[42] However, over the last few decades there has been an increase in sectarian tensions as Muslims—in one case Druze—have collectively attacked their Christian co-citizens and vandalized their property, in all cases without immediate Israeli police intervention. The most notorious case was a conflict between Muslims and Christians in Nazareth concerning the building of a mosque in front of the Catholic basilica on public land. In addition to violent attacks, Christians were condemned in the Friday sermons that were broadcast throughout the city on loudspeakers. As a result, Christians feel deeply betrayed by the event and many have begun to question where their true loyalty should lie. Regarding this incident Lybarger reports the conclusion of the Palestinian sociologist Bernard Sabella "that the 'old nationalist consensus' no longer existed and hence pan-Arabism or Communism or any of the other forms of secular collective Palestinian identity could [no longer]serve to reintegrate the nation."[43] The most visible sign of Muslim assertiveness in the city today are multiple billboards hung in public places with Islamic slogans and a huge banner that has been hung in front of the Catholic basilica with verses from the Qur'an condemning non-believers. The verses are changed every now and again. One example reads, "Whoever seeks a religion other than Islam, it will never be accepted of him, and in the Hereafter he will be one of the losers." During our stay in Nazareth we heard numerous comments from Christian Arabs that indicated a deep mistrust of their Muslim neighbors. Although rarely a topic of conversation, we have heard many phrases such as, "You don't know what you're doing in Europe letting in all those Muslims; they'll do to you what they do here," and "no Christian would rather live under a Muslim than a Jew." We will discuss concrete steps taken by Christians in response to this situation in §3 below.

41. Bowman, "Nationalizing," 209. See also Sabella, "Socio-economic Characteristics," 82–95.

42. See, for example, Emmett, *Beyond the Basilica*.

43. Lybarger, "For Church or Nation?," 792.

2.7.2. *Christians under the Palestinian Authority*

Following the Six Day War the Arab-Israeli conflict underwent a process of "Palestinization," as indigenous Arabs organized themselves politically to take matters into their own hands rather than depend on other Arab states. This new form of national consciousness also spread to the Arabs of Israel, particularly Christians, who up until that point had largely identified with Israel's mixed Arab-Jewish communist parties.[44] In 1974 the Palestinian Liberation Organization (PLO) came to be recognized by the Arab League as the official representative of the Palestinian people rather than Jordan, who finally rescinded their claims in 1988. In addition to providing a political voice and identity, a primary purpose of the new organization was the armed liberation of the whole of Israel-Palestine, a goal it sought to achieve using means many defined as terrorist. Since its establishment, Christians have distinguished themselves in the organization mainly as spokesmen, although they have been less involved in the military arms of the organization.[45] (The National Front for the Liberation of Palestine, a Marxist-Leninist group that joined the PLO, was founded by the secular Orthodox Christian George Habash. A number of countries consider it to be a terrorist organization.)

A major milestone in the Palestinian national cause was the First Intifada (1987–1993), a spontaneous uprising against harsh Israeli rule that was initially non-violent in nature until it was later co-opted by the PLO.[46] This conflict ended in 1993 with the Oslo Peace accords, in which the PLO promised to recognize the State of Israel and cease armed conflict while Israel promised a gradual disengagement from the territories and the facilitation of the creation of an independent Palestinian state. The process failed and a Second Intifada (2000–2005) started, this time far more violent than the first, particularly because of the high involvement of the Islamic group Hamas. Since then, Arafat has died and the Palestinian people voted Hamas into power. Conflict broke out with the result that Hamas now rules Gaza and Fatah the West Bank. Hamas is religiously obliged to seek the destruction of Israel; Fatah is committed to secularism and has recently renounced

44. See El-Assal, *Caught in Between*, an Anglican clergyman and leader of the nationalist movement, for a personal account of the development of Palestinian nationalism in Israel and its tensions with the Communist movement, which chose to identify with the international proletariat rather than a particular ethnicity.

45. Tsimhoni, "Palestinian Christians," 143.

46. This interpretation comes from Aburish, *Arafat*.

the use of violence. On the Israeli side, there has been a marked growth in antipathy towards Arabs and a loss of hope in the possibility of peace. The most recent response by the government has been to cordon off both Gaza and the West Bank by constructing a huge separation barrier. For the West Bank it roughly follows the 1949 armistice treaty line (the so-called "Green Line"), though to international outrage much of it is built inside Palestinian land and around many of the still-expanding illegal Jewish settlements. Although it has significantly reduced the number of suicide bombings in Israel, it is suffocating the Palestinian economy, has cordoned off the Palestinian people from important medicinal and economic resources in Israel, hindered free movement within the territories and *de facto* annexed further Palestinian land (although the authorities say the barrier is not permanent).

With the establishment of the Palestinian Authority Christians have found themselves in a system that is "secular democratic" but which uses Muslim *sharia* law as a primary source of legislation. During the first ten years of PA rule, "Palestinian institutions were ridden with corruption, incompetence, and a systematic misuse of economic funds and human resources. For a long time . . . the Palestinian Authority failed to establish a functioning legal system and a rule of law in the occupied territories."[47] Limitations placed upon the coercive power of the authority by the terms of the Oslo Agreement did not help matters. As a result, the PA enjoyed little trust and legitimacy among local Palestinians, who thus turned to more traditional institutions to regulate matters of justice. A primary institution is the patrilineal family clan, which can provide individual and family security. In order to stay in power and ward off potential competitors, Arafat took three measures to strengthen the clan system at the cost of government institutions: 1) he created an election law which enabled him to be constantly elected by obedient clan leaders. 2) He encouraged the use of the tribal law of *sulha* to resolve conflicts instead of the formal institutions of law enforcement. This method for seeking reconciliation aims to reestablish the status quo rather than punish perpetrators on an individual basis and so tends to work to the benefit of more powerful clans at the expensive of weaker clans and individual families. 3) He empowered clans by allowing for clan-based recruitment to his fourteen-odd security forces. With the collapse of PA institutions during the Second Intifada this process was accelerated.

47. Kaartveit, "The Christians of Palestine," 738. The following is primarily indebted to this excellent article.

Given the minority status of Christians and their less developed clan systems compared to Muslims, the ability of Christian families to achieve justice has been seriously weakened. This can involve matters such getting justice for loved ones killed in road accidents, rape, or even instances of daylight murder.[48] The biggest source of concern, however, is the Muslim theft of Christian land by means of forged documents.

Given that this imbalance of power also happens to fall along sectarian lines, Kaartveit notes how many Christians interpreted their afflictions in sectarian categories. They were being persecuted because they were Christians. He also noted, however, that Christian leaders would try to censure such interpretations because of the potential they held for creating inter-communal strife. Although Kaartveit does not rule out the religious dimension, he tentatively suggests that the lay leaders made a correct analysis of the situation.

Whereas the minority status of Christians and the traditional institutions of *sulha* and clan loyalty are certainly factors that lead to discrimination, it also appears to be clear that in the last few decades a more aggressive expression of Islam is gaining a foothold in both the territories and Israel (also see §2.7.1) and that this is the primary force leading to sectarian schism of a once more united people.[49] This dimension of discrimination on a religious basis is not only felt on the level of blatant injustice, it is experienced in everyday situations through demonstrations of disrespect or coercion.[50] Researchers have reported religiously inspired persecution such as vandalism of Christian institutions, public displays of disrespect, coercion to live according to Islamic mores (such as not smoking during Ramadan and wearing headscarves), graffiti threatening the extermination of Christians once the Jewish problem has been solved, unjust treatment by the police force which those involved say would never have happened to a Muslim, and so forth.[51] Often the persecution comes in the form of

48. See Kaarveit, "Christians of Palestine," for details. Weiner has a catalogue of crimes against Palestinian Christians under the PA in *Human Rights of Christians in Palestinian Society*. Some, however, feel that this author is partisan.

49. Lybarger discusses all these dimensions in her excellent article, Lybarger, "For Church or Nation?" Also see Bowman, "Nationalizing," who also blames part of the process on the insistence of foreign churches to define their Palestinian flock in religious rather than nationalist terms.

50. See Lybarger, "For Church or Nation?" in particular; Tsimhoni, *Christian Communities*; Tsimhoni, "Palestinian Christians"; Weiner, *Human Rights*.

51. The most extensive list of crimes can be found in Weiner, *Human Rights*.

continuous doubt about the genuineness of Christian commitment to the "Arab" cause, the assumption being that as followers of a "Western religion" Christians can only be secret Zionists or sympathizers with colonialism. For example, Tsimhoni describes the formidable non-violent resistance offered by the Christian inhabitants of Beit Sahur to the occupation during the First Intifada, which came at great cost to the community. Despite this, members of the Islamic movement hung up placards accusing the Christians of not contributing enough. One of them mocked the Christians for their alleged welcome of the Israeli conquerors with rice and sweets.[52]

Given the often conflicting reports between locals and researchers about the presence of inter-religious tension and Christian discrimination in the West Bank, we followed this inquiry up while interviewing local Christians on our travels through the West Bank. We found that the general response to questions about Christian-Muslim relations was positive: "we all get along very well here." Yet we also found that we had to read between the lines. Here are a few examples of conversation:

In a conversation with a priest and some lay members of the Greek Orthodox church in Ramallah, we were told that they had complete freedom of religion. We pointed out that according to the international definition, freedom of religion includes the right for *anybody* to choose his religion, but that according to *Sharia* law and also PA law it was only possible to convert *to* Islam, it was not possible to convert *from* it (see also chapter 6 in this book). They laughed and said, "Oh, that's the Western definition of freedom. We do things differently here. Nobody changes their religion." Curious as to whether this is indeed an "Eastern" definition rather than a capitulation of Arab Christianity to Islamic pressure, we pushed the issue with a Greek Catholic priest in Ramallah. The dialogue went like this:

> Q: "What do you do if a Muslim comes to you and asks to convert?"
>
> Ans: "I help him find Jesus in Islam and send him back."
>
> Q: "But what if he feels Jesus is far more visible in Christianity and so insists that he wants to stay in the church?"
>
> Ans: "Then I would send him to the Baptists."[53]
>
> Q: "Is it part of your church tradition not to accept converts?"

52. Tsimhoni, *Christian Communities*, 176.

53. At an earlier stage in the conversation he had said that Arab Baptists were not true Arabs because their religious was American.

> Ans: "This is just the way we do it . . . There are things we have to live with. You know that according to Islam you cannot convert. Maybe in his heart he converts but remains a Muslim in relation to society. There is no separation between religion and state. If he converts he will be estranged. Even the Christians would be confused because your religion is related to your tribe and the Arab is born into his religion."
>
> Q: "But the Pope baptized a Muslim."
>
> Ans: "That Egyptian guy, if he had true faith he would have been baptized in private."

A very different account of this issue was provided in two separate conversations by a Greek Orthodox deacon and a Greek Catholic Priest in Taybeh, the only remaining entirely Christian town in the West Bank. Both had experience of baptizing Muslim converts and both said they would have no qualms about doing so. This is because Christianity is a "better religion."[54] When asked about what Islamic law prescribes for such converts, Father Jack simply used his hand to make the sign of a knife cutting a throat. The deacon told us that more secular Muslim families were more tolerant and could let it pass.

Here is another statement of solidarity with Muslims that simultaneously revealed the experience of discrimination, this time made by the Arab Orthodox priest in Ramallah:

> Christians and Muslims have been good neighbors for a long time. I've been here for fifteen years and I've never faced problems. The same applies to my father and grandfather. This is true elsewhere as well. In the villages, this is different because they don't know what Christians are. They don't learn about this in school, this is the first problem that we face. In Ramallah, this is different, we know about each other.

The cosmopolitan nature of Ramallah shields many Christians, because Muslims have the advantage of getting to know them. Elsewhere, however, this is not the case, and so problems arise. We asked if the church

54. The Orthodox deacon told us the story of how a Muslim family from a neighbouring village killed their daughter because she had gotten pregnant out of wedlock by a married Christian man from Taybeh. We asked what Christians would do to if their daughter had gotten pregnant from a married Muslim man. He said that they might disown her, but it would be highly unlikely that they would kill her. He then told the story of Jesus forgiving the adultness in the Gospel of John and said that Christianity is a religion of love.

was doing anything to enlighten broader Muslim society and he responded that a long time ago they had asked Arafat to organize a conference between priests and sheikhs on live television so that people would be informed about Christianity. They also put pressure on him to change the school curriculum for the state schools, which only teaches about Islam but not Christianity. Unfortunately, no real meetings were held and the textbooks have not been changed. We also often heard that things are good *here*, not like *there*. In Bethlehem we heard that "relations are good here, not like in Nablus"; in Nablus we heard that "relations are good here, not like in Bethlehem."

The most explicit rejection of unity came from a very knowledgeable Greek Orthodox journalist and activist from Bethlehem. He first said that an originally nationalist conflict had become religious (on both the Jewish and the Arab side). Now "we Christians are living in a sandwich between two pieces of bread. Actually, today, our relations with the Jews are not so bad." The response of most Christians is "quietism" and they criticize him for revealing cases of Muslim abuses of Christians because they fear he will simply cause more trouble.[55] When asked how he felt about church leaders who speak of Muslims and Christians being one people he responded with an expletive that cannot be reproduced here. He went on to say, "They only care to maintain their privileges, doing nothing to help persecuted Christians, either abroad [he mentions Syria and Iraq], or at home." He refused to sign the Kairos Document (see §3.2 below) because it was one-sided, only critiquing the Israelis but not pointing out abuses at home. He then adds, "In a letter to [the bishops] I quoted the gospel of John, 'The truth will set you free.' I said, 'All you say about the occupation is correct. But the truth can't be portioned. Why don't you address internal affairs? You will say that it will be used by your enemies. I say, "even if the devil uses it, it doesn't matter."'" His favorite Bible verse is John 8:33: "you will know the truth and the truth will set you free."

***

We have now come to the end of our historical overview of Christianity in "the Holy Land." Throughout the analysis we have tried to keep an eye on its varying statuses and roles. In the next section we will focus more on the responses of contemporary indigenous Christians to the situation in which they find themselves. There is much that could be said. The Christian

55. The details he provided of abuses were not much different to those documented by Weiner in *Human Rights*.

churches are deeply ingrained into the lives of the traditional communities, not only providing for their spiritual needs but also—to varying degrees and with a greater or lesser clerical involvement —helping facilitate their communal life through the provision of educational and women's associations, youth work, scouts groups, and community clubs.[56] Furthermore, the Christian churches have provided numerous institutions that serve both the Christian as well as the Muslim community, such as schools, hospitals, vocational training colleges, and libraries.[57] One particularly context-sensitive project, for example, is the International Center of Bethlehem set up by the Lutheran pastor and theologian Mitri Raheb to provide work, training, and cultural development for both Muslims and Christians. Based on our interview with a key worker there, a key goal of the center is to "leaven" Palestinian society (our word) by instilling the virtues of tolerance and forgiveness. In fact, this "leavening" function was considered by a number of our interviewees to be a primary service the highly respected Christian schools offered to community. By instilling virtues such as discipline, respect, and mutual understanding Palestinian society as a whole was being made more humane. Our interviewees felt that the many Muslims who attended these schools (they often constitute the majority of the students) were aware of this contribution, which led them to respect the Christian presence in the region.

Despite this important facet of Christian service, given that such institutional activity is fairly characteristic of the church wherever one goes we have decided to focus here on those most salient examples of response to the contemporary situation which seem specifically particular to Palestinian(-Israeli) Christians. We have organized them into the following two categories, namely 1) emigration and the attempts to counter it; 2) acts of solidarity with the nation and/or the church. This twofold division, however, is simply heuristic, as many of these activities intersect.

3. CONTEMPORARY CHRISTIAN RESPONSES

The sources for our following analysis are both secondary literature, our own experience in Nazareth, an Arab city in Israel, as well as two weeks of field work in the West Bank interviewing clergy and laity from the Catholic

56. See the detailed study by Tsimhoni, *Christian Communities.*

57. Though a bit dated, a thorough overview of church institutions in the State of Israel can be found in Colbi, *Growth and Development.*

and Orthodox Churches about the challenges the community faced and how it might be responding. Interviews were held mostly in Arabic but also in English and Spanish. As things are in the Middle East, interviews were organized spontaneously on the day as we drove into the following locations: Bethlehem, Jericho, Nablus, Rafidia, Ramallah, Taybeh, and Zebabdeh.

3.1. Emigration As Response and Responses to Emigration

One way to exercise agency in response to suffering is to get up and leave. As mentioned above (§2.4), this has been a continuous Middle Eastern Christians strategy since the nineteenth century. Sabella estimates that between 1967 and 1999 35.3 percent of the Arab Christian population has left the West Bank, 15.8 percent of the entire population.[58] The once-Christian-majority towns of Ramallah and the Bethlehem area have now lost that majority, though other factors for the demographic shift are also responsible (higher Muslim birth-rate; influx of Muslim refugees; the redrawing of municipal boundaries).

Within Israel, a survey conducted in 1990 revealed that emigration among Christians was three times higher than among Muslims. Reasons given revolved around employment (38.6 percent) along with permanent emigration and family reasons (13.5 percent each).[59]

The secondary literature that discusses this phenomenon accords the primary motive for Christian emigration to the economy. As Sabella puts it, "People with a good and secure job will think twice before deciding to leave the country. Palestinians, including Christians, do not leave simply out of political or social frustration—they seem to have grown accustomed to these. They leave if they do not have opportunities to gain a livelihood, and in order to ensure some sense of stability in their own lives, and in those of their children."[60] Christians are particularly sensitive to this factor, as many of them are from the middle class and have a high education. Another factor that a few scholars have noted is sectarian violence of the kind discussed

58. Sabella, "Socio-economic Characteristics," 92. In surveys he conducted in in 1989 and 1990 , reasons for emigration were employment and permanent emigration (44.8 percent), family and marriage (34.1 percent), study (14.9 percent), and other reasons (4.4 percent).

59. Ibid., 94–95.

60. Ibid., 92–93.

above (§2.7) the spread of a more assertive Islam is causing people to leave.[61] This latter interpretation is hotly contested by Christian representatives of the community, who blame such theories on Zionist attempts to undermine the unity of the Palestinian people and direct attention away from the occupation, which they consider to be the real problem.[62] Our own field work does not support the thesis that religious tension is a reason for leaving, though it is not always easy to know given the reticence our interviewees often showed about talking about such tensions (see §2.7.2). Every one said that the number one challenge facing the Palestinian people is the economy, though complaints about travel restrictions were also common (not everyone put all the blame for the economic malaise on the occupation however; some mentioned bad local government, others the lack of natural resources, and a couple of priests complained about a culture of dependency among their constituency and lack of initiative).

Although we did not systematically research this question among Arabs in Israel, based on numerous conversations it seems clear that a significant reason why foreign countries such as America, Germany, and Jordan are so attractive—beyond the possibility of getting a better job and education—is that when there Arabs are not stuck in an ethnic or religious box which is then negatively evaluated. One man said that he is better off economically in Israel but better off psychologically in Jordan, because there nobody cares about his ethnicity. The emotional dimension was brought home in a conversation with an Arab Baptist from Tur'an, a village that had suffered Muslim attacks on Christians in the nineties. His pain was palpable as he described his disappointment at the failure of Arab nationalism, for who else could he identity with? His language, culture, identity, taste in music and food are those of the "Muslim" East and not the "Christian" or "Israeli" West, and yet this majority culture in the Middle East was increasingly rejecting Christians (the "Arab Spring" is still underway), and Israel appears to lack the ideological categories with which to affirm his presence.[63]

On our travels we identified three particularly noticeable Christian responses to this mass exodus: the provision of subsidized housing for young

61. This point is made by Weiner, *Human Rights*, and Tsimhoni, "Palestinian Christians."

62. See, for example, Sabella, "Socio-economic Characteristics."

63. As Avrum Ehrlich rightly points out, it is not enough for the state to grant its minorities economic and political freedoms, it must also find a way to make them feel that they are essential to its existence (see "Attitudes of Arab Christianity").

families, the creation of work opportunities, and the attempt to change the attitudes of local Christians.

The provision of subsidized housing for young (hopefully fertile) Christian couples has the purpose of keeping that segment of society which is vital for the future of the community, not only as adult contributors to society but also the producers of offspring (as mentioned above, Christians have a much lower birth-rate than Muslims). The Latin churches in particular excelled in this project. They currently have two buildings in the Bethlehem Governorate and are planning one in Rafidia. The Greek Catholics have done something along the same lines in Taybeh and the bishop of the very small Syriac Catholic Church told us that that his denomination was planning to partner with another Catholic group (perhaps the Franciscans, the Patriarchate, or the Greek Catholics) to build such accommodation in Jerusalem. The Latins also have a similar project in Nazareth, Israel. Typical of what has been said so far, the Greek-run Greek Orthodox appears little interested in such matters. When we asked an official at the Orthodox Society about this (an Arab lay organization that is in deep tension with the Greek ecclesial hierarchy), he said, "The land belongs to the church. The church belongs to the Greeks." They had apparently promised land for such a purpose thirty years ago but had not yet delivered. In Rafidia near Nablus the Orthodox Society and not the Patriarchate owned the land, so without any external help from the church hierarchy—for which we could sense a certain bitterness—they had taken matters into their own hands. Showing initiative and business acumen, they have started a number of projects to serve the community, including the provision of subsidized housing.

A second strategy was directed towards alleviating the economic situation, which does not necessarily have to do with reducing emigration but may alleviate it. Although one Greek Catholic priest felt that he could do no more than give a few donations at festival times, another priest from Zebabdeh near Jenin showed great industry and creativity in meeting the needs of his flock. After creatively reviving his Greek Catholic community that had been decimated by the First Intifada and rebuilding its destroyed property, this priest set out to meet the economic plight that had been aggravated by the construction of the nearby separation barrier. The locals could no longer sell all their olives, so he arranged for a friend from Bethlehem to teach locals how to make olive soap and sell it abroad; he also set up facilities and training to help local women do stich work as an extra source of income. For all these projects, he drew on outside contacts, which sought out and maintained on his own initiative (mostly Presbyterians from the US and Canada). Similar to the Orthodox in Rafidia, he felt abandoned by a complacent and disinterested hierarchy: "The bishop [in Haifa] hasn't sent me ten candles in the last year!"[64] Foreign led projects also abound. We visited a center in Bethlehem run by the Silesians for training locals in olivewood carving, thus creating skills for generating income.[65]

Both the priest form Zebabdeh and another Greek Catholic priest from Taybeh complained that this kind of initiative was rare among Palestinian Christians, who had grown accustomed to living on handouts and expecting their churches to provide for all their needs. This led to another response to the economic situation on the part of Abouna Jack from Taybeh: a ministry of liberation from the "inner occupation" (as he put it). Along with a number of interviewees we spoke to, he claimed that a major factor in the suffering of the people is their own sense of helplessness. Through preaching and teaching he encouraged his flock to draw their faith from God and take their lives into their own hands.

This ministry "to the mind" brings us to the final strategy we encountered to keep Christians in the land: a cultivation of their sense of "Arabness." At least for the purposes of our interview, the Greek Catholic priest in Ramallah defined his ministry to his people—by which he meant all Palestinians and not just Christians—exclusively in terms of his educating them about their true identity. They are all one nation, first Arabs and then only second Christians and Muslims. As such, "Christians" are not really a minority for there is no distinction between them and their Muslim brethren.[66] In fact, he went so far as to say that indigenous Jews before Zionism were also "Arabs," as this was their culture and language (he did add that Arab Baptists, of whom there are a few in Ramallah, are not "true Arabs," because they follow the ideology of an American religion). He laments that this understanding is waning among his people: "Before we

64. To be fair, this bishop has achieved fame for constructing a multi-ethnic and religious school in an Arab town in Israel, where he is also working on building an Arab university.

65. This practice was originally the fruit of Protestant mission to the Jews in the nineteenth century, as the Anglican and Lutheran missionaries found that Jews who converted soon lost their jobs. In response, Conrad Schick devised the technique of carving olivewood figures as an alternative source of income.

66. Thankfully, Christian distinctives were not completely disolved in nationalist categories. When asked what contribution Christians made to the overall Arab "mosaic," he said "belief in the resurrection of Jesus. Muslims don't have this."

called ourselves 'Arabs,' then 'Palestinians,' and today more and more we are defining ourselves as 'Christians' or, even worse, as Orthodox or Catholic." This, he says, is the result of American and Zionist influences—or even democracy. "Westerners come and tell the Christians they are minorities. . . . Here, especially in Ramallah, there are Western influences." This must be fought. By helping his flock understand that they are as Arab as their Muslim neighbors, they will feel like they belong and thus stop leaving. According to Abouna Abdulla, this sense of not belonging is a greater threat to the Christian population than the economic and political problems.

3.2. National and/or Religious Solidarity

During the first phase of Israel's existence, the foreign-dominated churches of Israel-Palestine remained neutral concerning political developments. Since 1967, however, all of the churches in Israel-Palestine that were not already considered national churches (such as the Armenians or the Ethiopians) or were not content to retain a particular ethnicity in power—as is the case with the Greek Orthodox church—underwent a gradual process of "Arabization." A highpoint was reached in the eighties with the appointment of a Palestinian, Michel Sabbah, as the Latin patriarch for Jerusalem. With this new indigenous leadership, the policy of neutrality was abandoned and church leaders took it as their God-given responsibility to "take the side of the oppressed" and advocate for their needs. The oppressed were understood to be the one, united, brotherhood of the Palestinian people—Christian and Muslim—and their need was an end to the occupation and the creation of an independent state alongside Israel (we are not aware of any Christian leader calling for the destruction of Israel). This united concern for the one people also had ecumenical ramifications unheard of in the Holy Land for centuries, as leaders began to formulate common statements on issues of politics and social justice and—eventually—even theology.[67] A

67. Tsimhoni, "Palestinian Christians," 144. In this connection it is worth pointing out the online article by Malcom Lowe, "Who Are the Heads of Churches in Jerusalem?", which is a highly critical—too scathing in our view—analysis of the development of this so-called common Palestinian theology. Despite its often unwarranted language (e.g., the description of the authors of the Kairos Document as "has-beens and wannabes"), contacts that we have in Jerusalem who do not share this author's "right of center Zionist point of view" feel that it has been extensively researched and elements may be in fact true. A brief summary in the article is as follows: "Something was written by somebody and sent to various people, then put out in the name of 'the churches in Jerusalem,'

significant example is the publication in 1987 of a strongly-worded joint statement signed by all "Heads of the Christian Communities in Jerusalem"—including the Greek Orthodox patriarch—describing the suffering of the Palestinians and protesting the activities of the Israeli authorities. It was addressed to the international community and called upon the UN to take action. Another significant document is the so-called "Kairos for Palestine" (2009). Modeled on the 1985 South African Kairos document, this ecumenical statement decries Israeli policies as well as Christian Zionist interpretation of the Bible, repeatedly advocates non-violent resistance, and calls for the international community to boycott Israel.[68]

In addition to bringing the plight of the Palestinians to the international community and calling for action, this new generation of indigenous Christian clergy also sought to minister to its flock pastorally by constructing a new "contextual Palestinian theology" that would offer hope, solace, and a plan for action.[69] The first move in this direction was the establishment of the Tantur Ecumenical Institute for Theological Studies, but the overly international and theoretical air disappointed some local theologians, who went on to set up the Al-Liqa' Center, an Arab language institute for Arabs, which sought to generate insights directly relevant to the needs of contemporary Palestinians. Two major fields of inquiry have been the construction of a common ecumenical Palestinian Christian identity, especially in terms of its relationship to the Palestinian national struggle, and the quest for Muslim-Christian unity. Muslims are routinely invited to the latter of conferences and most of what is said and thought at these events is directed to generating empathy and understanding among Muslims for the Christians.[70]

Two other institutes worth mentioning in this connection are the Sabeel Institute set up by the Anglican canon Naim Ateek to help him

---

whether or not the people contacted had even reacted to it." If this portrayal has any truth, the standard portrayal found above would have to be revised.

68. For a sympathetic interpretation of this contested document see Schmid, "Palestinian Christians."

69. This practical, ministerial function of much Palestinian theology has been highlighted and explicated in the masterful analysis of the movement by Gräbe, *Kontextuelle palästinensische Theologie*. Much less sympathetic Zionist responses can be found in Ehrlich, "Attitudes" and Nerel, *Anti-Zionism*. Briefer summaries can be found in Tsimhoni, *Christian Communities* and "Palestinian Christians."

70. Gräbe repeatedly points out ways in which the Muslim attendees have set the agenda, whether conscious or not, of much theology making dones in Al-Liqa'.

further develop a non-violent Christian theo-political approach towards the Israel-Palestine conflict (a "Palestinian liberation theology"), as well as the evangelical Bethlehem Bible College. Its dean, Salim Munayer, has set up the organization Musalaha, which aims to facilitate mutual understanding between Jewish and Palestinian teenagers. On the other hand, its Old Testament scholar Yohanna Katanacho is working on developing a mode of reading the Old Testament that both does justice to evangelical hermeneutics as well as the aspirations of the Palestinian people.[71] It is worth mentioning that there are Arab evangelicals who read the Old Testament in —for want of a better word—a more "Christian Zionist" (or perhaps "Dispensationalist") framework.[72] Often times, however this theology is undeveloped and considered insignificant compared to the more important themes of salvation through faith in Christ and a sanctified life (see chapter 5 in this book).

There is no single "Palestinian contextual theology," nor have any schools of thought developed. Rather, each theologian acts on his own initiative and independently of his denomination.[73] Nevertheless, it appears that much of what has been written has, on the whole, not found a positive reception in Western Christian and Jewish circles. Accusations include the following: unfair or distorted representation of events, lack of self-criticism (in that only Israel but never the PA or terrorists receive blame), distortion of the Bible by "Palestinizing" it and "de-Judaizing" it, neo-Marcionism, over-accommodating to Islam, illegitimately infusing political events with theological significance, etc. The cultural gap between East and West, the reality of post-Holocaust theology, and the very different cultural location of Western Christians/Israeli Jews and Palestinian Arabs has made communication between the two groups—of which there has been a lot over the years—very difficult.[74]

71. See Katanacho, *The Land of Christ.*

72. A very few examples can be found in Gräbe, *Kontextuelle palästinensische Theologie*, 170 and Nerel, "Anti-Zionism," 31–32.

73. Gräbe, *Kontextuelle palästinensische Theologie.*

74. See ibid. Concerning social location, it is worth citing Geries Khoury's response to criticism made by Western Christians: "Speaking from a Christian context of long-term minority existence, I first want to say, '*Do not despise the desire to survive*—as churches, as communities and as individuals'. It has not been easy to maintain Christian presence in the Holy Land and seeking confrontation at any opportunity could have led to the extinction of the Christian Church on many occasions" (222).

We thus have a case of *religious leaders* exercising solidarity with the Palestinian *nation*, but, as discussed above (§2.7), the unity of this nation itself has long started to crumble along sectarian lines with many laity turning back to their *religion* in rejection of a *national* idea they feel has failed them.[75] Although advocates of a secular Palestinian nationalism such as many of the theologians mentioned above still exist, in his field work in the West Bank between 1999 and 2000 Loren Lybarger has also identified what he calls a "religio-communal revitalization" and an "apolitical piety" as responses to the Islamicization of both Palestinian society and their struggle.[76] In the former, Christians are defining themselves in terms of their religion and distancing themselves from their Muslim neighbors. Whereas some do so in a superficial manner, such as publicly displaying crosses without getting involved in the life of the church, others want "to engage the Islamist threat directly by equipping themselves with a deeper command of their traditions, a readiness to engage in spirited apologetics, and stronger inter-Christian institutions."[77] The latter option shows no interest in the contemporary situation, seeking refuge in the "alternative reality" that has been discovered in the gospel (and mediated, for example, through the Orthodox liturgy).[78]

As outlined above when discussing the status of Christians in the West Bank (§2.7.2), our own research has also revealed the reality of Muslim persecution, but also the fact that there appears to be what we call "double-discourse," a discrepancy between what is said in public or to foreigners and what is said in private. Often positive statements about relationships between the two communities indirectly revealed signs of oppression. We also noted the repetition of certain arguments in order to ward of claims that perhaps relations were not so good: instances of persecution were only by "crazed" individuals or people motivated by money or pride; the rise in sectarianism as a Zionist or Western conspiracy foreign to the Arab mentality and only concocted in order to destroy it; one can be religiously free without having to have the freedom to choose one's religion. This strategy can also be seen as a form of Christian response to an existential threat, though its function has yet to be adequately determined. Our Bethlehem

75. See the relevant publications mentioned thus far by Tsimhoni, Ramon, Weiner, Lybarger, Bowman, Kaartveit, Gräbe.

76. Lybarger, "For Church or Nation?"

77. Ibid., 799.

78. Ibid., 802.

informant felt that silence on the part of the leadership was self-serving, in that pointing out injustices by Muslims and not only Israelis (he mentioned the Kairos Document as a glaring example) would not serve their purposes of maintaining power and influence. He also felt that the decision was strategic: conceding that the Palestinians were disunited would mean their enemies could use the information against them. Our Palestinian Israeli contacts said that Palestinians in the territories "have to" say such things because the backlash against them personally would be violent. Kaartveit felt that the interpretation of potential sectarian discrimination in terms of more accidental phenomena (the distribution of power) function to stave off growing sectarianism in the community as a whole. In an interview with a Bethlehemite, Bowman was told that Palestinians say such things to foreigners because the future is so uncertain they do not know what else they should say. Perhaps we should also entertain the possibility that "Arabists" such as our Greek Catholic contact in Ramallah truly do believe in the power of ethnic identity to contain and control religious differences.

Another strategic option not open to the majority of the Palestinians is application for Israeli citizenship. Tsimhoni notes that when peace talks with the Israelis accelerated during 1994, there was a burst in the number of applications for Israeli citizenship from Palestinians residing in East Jerusalem, a considerable number of whom were Christians. "Off the record, Christian applicants explained their motive as emanating from the uncertainty of the future under the Palestinian autonomy which was liable to be greatly influenced by traditional-fundamental Islam. By applying for Israeli citizenship, they hoped to obtain double security. Both Christians and Muslims expressed their hope for greater economic and employment opportunities, more freedom of travel, guarantees for civil rights, and social and health services by obtaining both Israeli and Palestinian citizenship."[79]

As a result of the sectarian tensions mentioned above (§2.7.1), similar patterns are developing among Arabs in Israel. Merav Mack, for example, cites research into acculturation orientations of the members of the Christian minority which "shows a growing sense of in-group Christian identity and separation from both the Jewish and the Muslim hegemonic societies" (he notes that the first survey in 2007 indicated greater identification with Jews; a second one in 2010 indicated a tendency of separation).[80] Another

79. Tsimhoni, "Palestinian Christians," 147.

80. Mack, "Christian Palestinians," 289, and n. 31. He is citing Horenczyk/Munayer's 1999 article "Acculturation Orientations." The 2010 survey is unpublished.

development is the rise in voluntary Christian recruits to the Israeli Defence Force (in 2013 the number of new recruits rose from thirty-five to about one hundred; there are currently about five hundred doing national service).[81] When asked why they join, their terminology includes expressions such as "patriotic duty," "fighting for my homeland," "giving back to society."[82] Mack cites other opinions by researchers who theorize that the motivating factor is their experience as un-armed Christians of intercommunal violence in mixed villages.[83] Such recruits now have the spiritual guidance of the Arab Greek Orthodox priest Gabriel Naddaf, who is actively encouraging his flock to abandon Palestinian nationalism, affirm their Christian identity, and pledge loyalty to the State of Israel. Together with a number of other Arab Israeli Christians, he recently held a conference in Jerusalem with the title, "Israeli Christians: Breaking Free? The advent of an independent Christian voice in Israel." The attendees claimed that their true ethnicity was "Aramaic" rather than "Arab" (they claim that Arab culture was imposed on them by Muslim invaders),[84] that they had time and again been betrayed by Muslims (references were made to the fate of Lebanon and the recent Arab Spring), and that the time had come to integrate into Israeli society, to "pay our dues and demand our rights."[85]

4. CHRISTIANITY AND FREEDOM IN ISRAEL-PALESTINE

All that remains to do now is tie the threads together by summarizing Christianity's status, response to pressure, and role in the region.

Israel-Palestine set the stage for the salvific events that constitute the very being of the church, and yet the church's institutional and dogmatic evolution with its attendant fragmentation into denominations all took place outside of the land. There never has been a completely "indigenous"

81. Lis, "Netanyahu."

82. Mack, "Christian Palestinians," 290.

83. Ibid. He refers, for example, to McGahern, *Palestinian Christians.*

84. This strategy of redefining oneself as Aramaic rather than Arab in order to better integrate in Israeli society can also be found in certain Maronite villages in the north of Israel, such a Gish. Members of the Gish community have even started a program with government funding to revivify the Syriac language.

85. In response to the statement that Christians are not afforded all their rights, Captain Bishara Shlayan replied, ""That may be," he said, but "you have to begin by pledging loyalty to your country and serving it. I believe that." For more detail, go here: http://www.israelhayom.com/site/newsletter_article.php?id=12341.

church of the Holy Land. Almost from the outset, with the exception of the earliest apostolic period, the various ecclesial manifestations of Christianity that have gained a foothold in the region have been configured in terms of cultural and political affiliations that are located elsewhere (Latin; Greek; Syriac; Coptic; Ethiopian; Georgian; Anglican; Lutheran; Russian; Chaldean). Yet, as an eschatologically oriented religion birthed by the penetration of eternity into concrete and particular time and space, throughout history this strip of land has retained an almost sacramental significance for almost all branches of Christendom (including many anti-sacramental yet highly apocalyptic free-church evangelicals). The result is that it has not only provided a home for almost every major denomination, its geography and sacred buildings have continued to be objects of international Christian interest. The results have often been beneficial for locals in terms of the money brought by pilgrims, the institutions established near the sites, and the leverage offered by the powerful patrons of the various denominations in securing better rights. Yet foreign interest has also often side-lined the needs of locals in its passion to tap into a holiness that should serve its own ends. In the present time, many indigenous Christians have directed this accusation towards the Greek Orthodox hierarchy and Christian Zionists, whose apparent lack of concern for their indigenous "brothers" has generated a backlash of self-assertion, both institutional and theological.

Local Christians have always been oppressed in one way or another by the region's various overlords, whether by other more powerful denominations (Syriacs by Byzantines; Byzantines by Latins) or by Islam. The contemporary form of secular democracy appears to be the system most able to provide Christians with the opportunity to flourish, contribute to civic life, and shape their destiny. This explains their passionate commitment to the cause and the large contribution—both politically and recently even theologically—that they have made towards it. Unfortunately, apart from the brief respite under the British, the likelihood of there being such a regime in the region appears to be diminishing. Although the State of Israel has striven to embody such a system, the ambiguity of its simultaneous desire to be Jewish coupled with the radicalization of many of its Jewish citizens in response to the ongoing conflict with Arabs is making it increasingly difficult for such a goal to be realized. On the Palestinian side, the Islamicization of society and the constant suspicion that Christianity is really a "Western" phenomenon is squeezing Christians out of the spheres of influence and power, spheres they often helped construct in the first place.

In early times, the only response that could be offered to oppression was conversion to the dominating religion. From the nineteenth century onwards, many have chosen to simply emigrate and live in Christian dominated regions such as North and South America, Europe, and Australia. The result has been the decimation of the community, with many considering its actual extinction a real possibility. As mentioned, another response that developed in the same period was the attempt to construct a secular state—or at least an inevitably Islamicized state that does not require the status of *dhimmitude* from its monotheistic minorities. With the waning hope in the secularism and nationalism they helped propagate, there appears to be a growing trend of Christians realigning themselves with their religious rather than national communities. An evangelical variety on this theme is to actually seek the conversion of Muslims to Christianity, though this is still very much a minority option (see chapter 6 in this book).[86] In Israel, there are indications—small but growing—that Christians are opting to identify with the Jewish state as a means to gain equality while preserving their Christian identity.

Researchers repeatedly point out that the contribution of Christians to their society far outweighs their numbers. Given their higher levels of education and familiarity with the culture of the West, Christians have provided the Arab community with businessmen, politicians, theologians, and advocates for the cause of the nation as a whole. A striking characteristic of Palestinian(-Israeli) Christian thought and practice has been its concern for the nation as a whole, regardless of sectarian loyalties. The numerous schools, hospitals, cultural and training centers are open to all with the purpose of providing for the material welfare of the community. As we have seen, there is even the unspoken hope that such institutions can also provide for the "spiritual" welfare of the nation through the inculcation of virtues that may be described as implicitly though never explicitly "Christian" (to do so would be to encourage the kind of sectarianism that is so threatening to Christians living among Muslims). In a sense, this attempt to leaven society may be seen as a contemporary form of "evangelism," given that the attempt to convert non-Christians is all but non-existent in Palestinian society. One question we constantly asked our informants in the West Bank was, "How would your society be different if Christians disappeared?" Not everyone provided a coherent answer, but we feel that the following two samples succinctly affirm a sense that Christian faith and practice is

86. For a rather dramatic recent example, see Yousef, *Son of Hamas*.

intrinsically good for society: "our ideas would disappear"; "there would be no belief in the resurrection."

CHAPTER 2

An Introduction to the Convention of Evangelical Churches in Israel (CECI)

by Azar Ajaj and Philip Sumpter

In 2005, representatives from five Christian denominations in Israel—Baptists, Assemblies of God, Open Brethren and Church of the Nazarene (the latter including a smaller denomination within them, the Christian Missionary Alliance)[1]—formed a coalition in order to make a bid with the Israeli government to gain recognition as an "official religion," a unified entity entitled to the same rights and responsibilities as Israel's other officially recognized religions. The purpose for seeking such a status was primarily practical, for non-recognition by the government inhibits the day-to-day functioning of individual congregations. However, the criteria required by the Israeli government for recognition as a single "recognized community" ("*'edah moqeret*") have confronted the federation with a number of challenges, especially given the diverse theologies represented by its five

1. The word "denomination" is not generally used by the Arab evangelicals in Israel, who prefer the term 'ecclesial family' (in Arabic: *'a'ilah kanasiyah*). There are a number of reasons for this: for some there is a theological concern for the identity of the true church, for others it is due to the fact that they are not recognized as official "denominations" (*'edot mokarot*) by the Israeli government, for others still there is simply a lack of awareness that their particular, extremely small church is part of a broader, world-wide organization. For example, there are not more than 120 Nazarenes in Israel, many of whom cannot speak English and have no connection with the broader denomination. For the sake of clarity, however, I will use the term in this article

constituent members. With these challenges have also come opportunities, however, both practical and theological in nature. Practically, for example, these churches are learning to pool their resources and conceive of themselves as a common identity. Theologically speaking, they are learning to ask what it means for the body of Christ to be one.

The name of this federation is the Convention of Evangelical Churches in Israel (CECI; referred to by locals in Arabic as the "*majma* ʿ," i.e., "convention"), and this article tries to tell its story.[2] Before we start, however, it is necessary to clarify two important elements of the CECI's identity, namely its self-designation as "evangelical" as well as the fact that it consists almost entirely of Arabs.[3]

After this clarification we will sketch the local context out of which the CECI grew. This will be followed by a discussion of its structure and constitution. Azar Ajaj, as a member of the executive committee, will add some personal reflections on some of the achievements of the CECI as well as some challenges that lie ahead.

EVANGELICAL AND ARAB

According to the self-understanding of the representatives of the five denominations that constitute the CECI, the most significant factor that binds them together is their evangelical confession; in other words, it is their commitments as denominations to "evangelical faith" that binds them into a unity. This commitment at the level of the denomination as a whole distinguishes them from the only officially recognized Protestant denomination in the country, the Episcopalian church, which may contain evangelicals but does not define itself as a church as evangelical.[4] The

2. The official Arabic language website can be found here: http://enjeely.org/. Dale Gavlak has published a brief introduction to the project in "Evangelical Collective."

3. A constituent member is the Alliance of Baptist Churches (ABC) which is open to all Baptists in the country. At present two Filipino churches are registered members. These churches, however, do not participate in the life the CECI

4. We are grateful to Phil Hill for this insight. Although the official title of this church is the Evangelical Episcopal Church, Diocese of Jerusalem, the general opinion among members of the CECI is that the clergy of this church are "liberal" rather than "evangelical." The Lutheran church, which is only found in the West Bank, also contains the word evangelical in its title: it is the Evangelical Lutheran Church in Jordan and the Holy Land. This church is also held by most members of the CECI to be "liberal" rather than "evangelical."

self-awareness of these churches as "evangelical," however, is oral rather than creedal. Nowhere is there a document that specifically defines what evangelical is. It is perceived to be common knowledge by those who are on the inside. When asked, the most common answer is that what makes one evangelical is a personal faith in the redemption wrought by the cross resulting in new birth, coupled with the desire to share this faith with others (i.e., to "evangelize"); there is also mention of the centrality of Scripture and a free style of worship (i.e., non-liturgical). With the exception of the Closed or Plymouth Brethren (see below), the five member denominations of the CECI are the only denominations in the country for whom these tenets are foundational to their identity.[5] When referring to evangelicals in this article, then, we have in mind the member denominations of the CECI, in addition to the Closed Brethren.[6]

An unofficial characteristic of the Convention is that it is entirely Arab, with Arabic being the means of all internal communication. This, however, is not an official policy of the Convention, nor does it desire to remain purely Arab. It is due to the fact that the indigenous evangelical population of Israel is either Arab or Jewish Messianic. Although the two groups do work together in various contexts in an unofficial capacity (see below), in general the latter group prefers to not be *officially and publicly* identified as Christian, let alone evangelical (there is, however, diversity of opinion on this issue in Messianic Judaism, which is a movement rather than a unified denomination). For example, even if a particular Messianic congregation is entirely Baptist in its theology, the church would not want to identify itself as "Baptist." A primary reason for this stance is their desire to emphasize the Jewishness of their identity to Jewish Israelis rather than their Christianess, which is perceived by the majority of Jewish Israelis to be foreign to Judaism and even a source of anti-Semitism.

5. It is precisely these tenets which distinguish evangelical Arabs from many of the theologians involved in what has been called "contextual Palestinian theology." For an excellent overview, see Gräbe, *Kontextuelle palästinensische Theologie*.

6. We will spell "evangelical" with a small "e," as per convention. If the CECI does succeed in gaining recognition by the government, it would presumably have to be spell with a capital.

ARAB EVANGELICALS IN ISRAEL

Arab evangelicals in Israel are a small minority. In fact, it is more accurate to say that they are a minority within a minority within a minority. As Arabs, they form 20.6 percent of the whole population of Israel.[7] As Christians they constitute only 10 percent of the Arabs in Israel, numbering around one hundred and sixty thousand individuals.[8] As Evangelicals, the number is no more than five thousand.[9] On each one of these levels, evangelical Arabs are faced with a number of different challenges. As Arabs, they must often struggle to achieve equal treatment with their Jewish co-citizens.[10] As Christians, there is a fear of oppression from Islam, especially with the rise of more radical Islamic governments in the Middle East.[11] As evangelicals, they can be subjected to verbal attacks from the traditional churches (such as the various Catholic and Orthodox churches), who often associate them with Zionists, Jehovah Witnesses, and various other non-Christian movements (see below).[12]

The various churches that constitute the CECI amount to thirty-five individual congregations,[13] the vast majority of them (thirty-one churches)

7. See Central Bureau of Statistics: http://www.cbs.gov.il/www/yarhon/b1_h.htm. The whole population currently stands at 7,968,000.

8. See Central Bureau of Statistics: http://www.cbs.gov.il/reader/newhodaot/hodaa_template.html?hodaa=201211349. It is worth noting that 80 percent of all Christians in the country are Arabs.

9. This is a rough estimate based on the average number of the church members combined with an estimated number of children in all the churches.

10. Although Arabs formally have equal rights in Israel, they do not always have access to these rights. This is a generally recognized fact within Israel and often features within the political programs of Jewish parties. A few examples suffice to illustrate the situation: Arab schools are underfunded in relation to Jewish schools; businesses invest more in Jewish population centers, reducing the possibilities of Arab employment; the pervasive presence of the military in industries such as aeronautics further inhibits the possibility of Arab employment; military service is often made a requirement for jobs in which no military experience is actually necessary; Arabs have a harder time buying property in areas predominantly populated by Jews, etc.

11. This materialized, for example, when Muslim and Druze mobs attacked Christian residents in Kufr Yasif, Jouls, Rama, Toraʿan and Nazareth. See, for example, the Hebrew language news article at http://www.haaretz.co.il/misc/1.1511638.

12. Some evangelicals believe that these churches feel threatened by the vibrant and attractive way of evangelical life, which is attracting members of its flocks.

13. Baptist Churches 16, Assemblies of God 7, Church of the Nazarene 3 (one of them is the Christian Missionary Alliance in Jerusalem), Open Brethren 4. These numbers are taken from the 3rd annual report book published by the Convention 2012, p.

being concentrated in the northern part of Israel, i.e., in Galilee and Haifa, with only three in the Tel Aviv area and one in Jerusalem.[14] Most of these churches have relatively few members, averaging between fifty to sixty persons; in a few churches the number of members does not exceed fifteen people. Having said this, there are two or three churches that have close to one hundred members. These statistics only apply to church membership, however. The number of people who attend church services in most of these churches is much larger than the number of official members.

As religious bodies, a decisive factor affecting the ability of these churches to operate is the system adopted by the Israeli government for regulating relations between the state and the country's various religious groups.[15] In short, Israel has granted a select number of officially recognized religious communities (Judaism, Christianity, Islam, the Druse faith and the Baha'i Faith) juridical autonomy in the area of personal status and family law (e.g., marriage and divorce; burial), a function that in Israel can only be fulfilled by one of these religious bodies.[16] The state distinguishes furthermore between ten officially recognized Christian "denominations" or "recognized communities" (*'edot mokarot*) (Roman, Armenian, Maronite, Greek, Syriac, and Chaldean Catholic Churches; the Eastern Orthodox Greek Orthodox Church; the Oriental Orthodox Syriac Orthodox Church; the Armenian Apostolic Church; Anglicanism), each of whom bear juridical autonomy for their members. The problem for the aforementioned evangelical free churches is that they are not recognized by the government as *'edot mokarot*, either individually or as a corporate body.

The lack of official recognition as a Christian "denomination" or "sect" has led many evangelical churches to register themselves as non-profit organizations (*amutot*). Although this solution enables them to engage in the tasks necessary for the day-to-day functioning of the church (e.g., opening bank accounts, paying salaries etc.), there are also some limitations.

71–75. One can add to this the 5 Closed Brethren Churches who are not members of the convention. I will provide more details about this phenomenon later.

14. Annual Report, 71–75.

15. This arrangement was by adopted by the newly formed State of Israel from the British, who themselves had developed it from the so-called "Millet System" of the Ottoman Empire.

16. Israel does not issue civil marriage, for example (though it does recognize it). When two secular Israeli Jews marry each other, the ceremony must be conducted by an Orthodox rabbi. Christians must be married by representatives of their officially recognized churches.

According to Israeli law, for example, a person receiving a salary from a non-profit organization is not allowed to be involved in its decision making process. As a result, pastors who receive their salaries from these churches cannot, legally, be one of the decision makers. Another issue is that, as *amutot*, individual churches and para-church organizations find it very difficult to get long-term visas for voluntary workers and missionaries from abroad. The most serious issue is that the status of non-profit organization does not give the church the right to deal with the aforementioned personal status issues such as marriage, divorce, and burial.[17]

These organizational factors were a primary motivation for some evangelical church leaders to seek to change the legal status of their churches from individual *amutot* to an *ʿedah moqeret*. Given that such a change in status would have a better chance of success with the Israeli government if the various denominations combined to form a unified front, working together was more desirable than each denomination going it alone. But a further advantage of working together was also identified: it would improve their visibility and legitimacy vis-à-vis their Israeli neighbors. Traditional Christians, Muslims and Jews often express confusion at the plethora of churches and denominations that are all nevertheless called "evangelical." This diminishes their authority and coherence, for they are not perceived to be a single body. Rather they are simply groups of individuals with little that binds them together. A single organization would thus lend substance to the claims of the individual churches that they are indeed one body in faith and practice and thus need to be taken seriously by the broader society.

We will now to give a brief overview of the history of this organization, from its inception in 2003 until the end of the year 2012.

17. The state did allow evangelical churches to issue marriage certificates at one point in the past. However, due to complications that arose when some couples attempted to get divorced, a right that was not given to evangelicals, the government informally decided to issue no more certificates (this change is policy is not documented anywhere). It is not true that Arabs have to leave the country to get married (as reported by Moon, "Christians Fight"). In order to divorce, couples need to change their denomination, usually to the Orthodox Church since the process is less complicated there. Burial is more complex. In Nazareth, for example, the Baptists have a recognized graveyard, so this is not an issue. Other cities have unspecified graveyards where anyone can be buried. In those places with only denominationally affiliated graveyards, the families will go to the church from which they had originally converted (assuming they are not originally from a Muslim background) in order to get permission to bury their loved ones.

THE FOUNDING OF THE CECI

The original initiative for the founding the convention should be attributed to Mr. Monther Naum, a nutrition engineer from Shefa-ʿAmr (in Hebrew, Shfarʿam) who is an elder in the Baptist church there.[18] He first shared his vision with several pastors and leaders who responded positively to his idea. After a few months of preparation and consultation with a wider group of evangelical leaders,[19] it was decided to involve all evangelical churches and institutions in further discussion. For this purpose, a conference was held in a conference center in Kibbutz Gonen between 19th and 23rd of September 2003. More than fifty representatives from all the evangelical churches, with the exception of the Closed Brethren, as well as leaders from para-church organizations came together to discuss the idea of establishing a single body that would represent all evangelicals in Israel.[20]

The majority of the participants agreed in principle that such an organization was needed and the name "Convention of Evangelical Churches in Israel" was agreed upon.[21] Beyond this initial step, a plan for further preparatory work was needed. The representatives set up three committees to present their recommendations for the next meeting.[22] The committees were as follows:

1. A committee to determine the constitution.
2. A committee to determine the statement of faith.
3. A follow-up and wording committee.

Over the next eight months, the committees held several meetings. Once a statement of faith and a constitution had eventually been proposed, it was time to call for a general assembly to discuss and approve the proposal.

On May 20th 2004 a general assembly was held at the Baptist School auditorium in Nazareth. After a day's discussions involving all the representatives, a statement of faith that obligates all members was accepted and

18. Mr. Monther Naum became the first chairman of the convention and later became the general secretary. For the last six years, he has also served as the chairman of the Association of Baptist Churches (ABC).

19. See, for example, the minutes of the preparatory meeting on May 29th 2003.

20. The Annual Report 2010, 23.

21. Minutes of general meeting, September 19th–23rd 2003.

22. Ibid.

signed.[23] As far as we have been able to determine, there were not any major theological disputes during this process. A few days later, on June 24th, the constitution was officially accepted at another general assembly of all the representatives.[24] (The constitution was revised a few years later, changes which were approved in the general assembly on May 15th 2010.[25] According to Mr. Aziz Daeem, the second chairman of the CECI who was responsible for the revision, the changes were primarily a matter of structure and style. As we will see below, there was a revision in content in relation to eschatology).

Finally, the Convention of Evangelical Churches in Israel was established on April 16th 2005 in the village of Shfa-ʿAmr. The ceremonial gathering involved over five hundred invitees and delegates from all the evangelical churches and para-church organizations along with many guests.[26]

While almost every single evangelical church in Israel is either a member of the convention[27] or is seeking to attain membership,[28] it is important to note that the only church group which did not join the convention was the Closed Brethren. The five churches constituting this denomination did not give an official reason for not joining. Azar Ajaj personally inquired into this matter, but did not receive a straightforward answer. Some expressed their preference for carrying on their ministry freely without having any kind of organizational attachment. Others claimed there was no agreement among the different leaders, and even that they had never met to discuss the matter so that no definite stance could be taken. In our opinion, there may also be theological concerns at stake, since Closed Brethren do not like to be called a "denomination" and do not feel that they can associate with all of the member denominations of the CECI. Nevertheless, the Convention has sought from the outset to maintain good relations with them. This

23. See the minutes of this meeting from May 20th 2004.

24. See the minutes of this meeting from May 24th 2004

25. Annual Report 2012, 27.

26. Annual Report 2010, 23. See also the minutes of this General Assembly.

27. As stated in the Annual Report 2012, 71–76, there are 30 churches and 11 para-church organizations that are registered members.

28. Membership is available only for churches who are members in one of the four denominations. We are currently aware of only two Baptist churches that are seeking membership. They must first be accepted by the Association of Baptist Churches in Israel before they can be accepted by the CECI. For now they only have observer status.

can be seen in the careful wording of the following statement from the first annual report:

> *We want to bring to your attention that the Churches of the Closed Brethren are not officially represented in the Convention and this according to their choice. Nevertheless, they are our brothers and sisters and a relation of love and respect binds us together. They have a blessed ministry and an important role in the evangelical ministry in our country, and they have not been included in the list of the churches of the Convention for organizational reasons only.*[29]

Application for the status as an *ʿedah moqeret* is a time consuming and challenging process. For this reason, the CECI did its work unofficially from the time of its establishment in 2005 until 2009. However, as the convention grew in size and significance there was a need for it to become legally registered. An application was sent to the government of Israel for the legal status of non-profit organization (*amuta*), which was granted on September 6th 2009.[30] The CECI has retained the status of *amuta* to this date.

STATEMENT OF FAITH

The function of a statement of faith is to provide an official account of the faith of the members of an organization. For this reason, it is necessary that all members agree with the content of the statement. Given the various denominations represented within the CECI, there were two theological challenges in particular, namely the issue of eschatology and the role of the Holy Spirit.

Concerning the Holy Spirit, the Open Brethren claim that miracles ceased with the early church whereas the charismatic Assemblies of God consider the Spirit's ongoing miraculous activity to be of central importance. In order to accommodate both views, the statement of faith simply adopted the relevant article from the Nicene creed, which is open enough to accommodate all positions: "I believe in the Holy Spirit, the Lord, the giver of life, who proceeds from the Father, who with the Father and the Son is adored and glorified, who has spoken through the prophets ."[31]

29. Annual Report 2010, 24 (translation mine).

30. Annual Report 2011, 40

31. Annual Report 2011, 47. Although most Western evangelicals adopt the "*filioque* clause" ("and the Son") in the Nicene Creed, evangelicals in Israel decided not to include

Concerning the issue of eschatology, some churches are dispensationalist, others are amillennialist, and still others are not particularly concerned either way.[32] The original statement of faith contained many terms that are typical of premillennialist views of the End Times, such as the rapture, tribulation and the millennium.[33] However, due to the presence of amillennialists in the CECI, these terms were dropped in a later revision and replaced with the more general language of the second coming, judgment, resurrection of the dead.[34] This brings the confession, once again, into conformity with the traditional church creeds.

THE CONSTITUTION

Whereas the statement of faith outlines the core beliefs of the convention's members, the constitution concerns more organizational matters such as management of finances, guaranteeing appropriate representation of members in the executive committee,[35] the formulation of a common vision and the development of structures for implementing that vision.

An interesting and important section in the constitution is §3, which sets out four goals the Convention hopes to achieve.[36] The CECI aims

1. to represent the evangelical church and its members to the state, thereby guaranteeing the civil rights of all of its members, as is done for the other denominations and religions in Israel;

---

this later addition. This phrase was added in 587 AD at a local council in Toledo, and was later adopted by the Western Church. It was this addition that contributed to the great schism between the Eastern and Western Church in 1054 AD. One reason for the omission by evangelicals in Israel may be that many of them originate in the Orthodox Church. The issue, however, was never discussed and the decision to omit it does not appear to have been doctrinal in nature.

32. In short, Premillennialists believe that the final judgment will be preceded by a thousand year reign of Christ on earth, which involves a timetable of specific events such as a rapture of the church and a tribulation for those who remain. Amillennialists believe that the biblical image of the thousand year reign is a symbol for the current life of the church.

33. Annual Report 2010, 31.

34. Annual Report 2011, 50

35. See Annual Report 2011, 64–65. For details, see our section on challenges for the future below.

36. Annual Report 2011, 54–55 (translation mine).

2. to strengthen and deepen relationships among the evangelical churches;
3. to develop, coordinate and support evangelical work, including humanitarian ministries of a charitable, social, educational, cultural and creative nature (the latter including art, theatre and Christian literature);
4. to establish and develop relations and/or partnerships with other conventions, churches and national and global bodies, all to the glory of the Lord.

Whereas the original *rasison d'être* for the CECI is contained in point 1, we can see how the establishment of the organization, whether recognized as an *ʿedah mokeret* or not, raises other potential advantages for the churches.

With limited resources and staff who work on a voluntary basis, it is almost impossible to meet all of these goals in a relatively short time. For this reason, a decision was made to invest in the first two points listed above, that of achieving recognition of the CECI by the state as an *ʿedah mokeret* and that of achieving greater cooperation amongst the convention's member bodies. To this we now turn.

CURRENT PRIORITIES

First, an attempt was made for the Convention to be recognized as an *ʿedah mokeret* by the government, a move which would effectively transform the individual church denominations into a single "denomination" in the eyes of the government. The first task was to persuade the Assemblies of God, the Evangelical Alliance of Israel and the Baptist Convention in Israel not to attempt to become "recognized communities" on their own, but rather to submit an application as part of the broader body of the CECI. One of the reservations these denominations had about joining the CECI was a possible impact on their property rights and the ability to run their own affairs as individual denominations. These concerns have been satisfactorily dealt with and they have all agreed to join the Convention. In this they were successful.[37] A general secretary was officially appointed whose

37. Interview with Mr. Butros Mansour, the CECI lawyer for the issue of recognition. on January 15, 2013 (Moon wrongly claims that the Christian Alliance have made a separate application, in "Christians Fight," 18).

primary task was to follow up on this issue.[38] Two lawyers were hired, one to prepare all the required documents and another one to deal with legal the requirements and further development of the case. Last but not least, two committees, a theological and a legal committee, were formed to compose a Personal Status Law for the Evangelical Ecclesial Court, the function of which is to oversee the issues of marriage and divorce mentioned above. An ecclesial court is a requirement of the government, and composing its legal framework has raised theological challenges for the CECI. Questions which must be answered are, for example: when can one divorce? Can one re-marry after divorce? The challenge consists in composing a law that will satisfy all the CECI's constituent denominations. Rather than trying to appease all the viewpoints found in the denomination, however, the committee has decided to engage in fresh theological work, turning to the Bible or order to develop policy from first principles.[39]

An application for recognition was sent to the Office of the Prime Minister on August 2011, along with a letter signed by leaders of Western churches and para-church organizations.[40] The CECI did not have any illusion that this request would be positively received by the state. As was expected, a year and half later the CECI received a response from the Prime Minister's Office declining the request.[41] Their justification was as follows:

> There are many other groups that are seeking governmental recognition and in view of the situation the office of the Prime Minister does not find it right for the time being to change the status quo. The office of the Prime Minister highly estimates the implementation of the law of religious freedom and worship in the State of Israel. Non-recognition of any group as a religious denomination does not prevent it from practicing its religious freedom and worship (translation by Azar Ajaj).

This letter will form the basis for an appeal by the lawyers of the CECI, who will argue, among other things, that it contains a contradiction: if our

38. Minutes of executive committee from June 11, 2012.

39. Phil Hill of Nazareth Evangelical Theological Seminary has published his contribution in "Do Jesus and Paul Agree?".

40. Interview with Mr. Butros Mansour, the CECI lawyer for the issue of recognition. On January 15, 2013.

41. See letter from Prime Minister office to CECI lawyer dated 10th of December 2012.

churches are not able to marry people, then how are they free to practice their religion (especially as there is no such thing as civil marriage in Israel)?

The second prioritized goal was that of strengthening the fellowship and joint ministries of pastors, leaders, and members of the different member churches. This is arguably a valuable task for all church denominations given the theological significance of unity in Christ. The small and vulnerable nature of the evangelical community in Israel has helped serve as an impetus in getting different churches to talk to each other, pray for each other, and pool resources.[42] A perusal of the summary of all the convention's activities over the last eight years reveals the efforts that have been invested in achieving this goal.[43] Within this period, the CECI has either organized or supported a monthly pastors' breakfast, training conferences for leaders, annual Christmas celebrations, and has sponsored its members' various ministries, outreach campaigns and national prayer days. For the coming year (2013) the major emphasis will be on strengthening our common youth ministry through training seminars and events to bring together youth in the country.

Many of the church laity have responded to these programs with the complaint that they focus too heavily on church leaders and not on the average person in the pew. The executive is taking these complaints seriously and is actively planning to offer conferences and various programs that will bring different church members together, both on a regional as well as on a national basis.

ACHIEVEMENTS AND POTENTIAL FUTURE CHALLENGES

Although the CECI has not yet achieved its original and primary goal, recognition as a religious community by the Israeli government, we can mention at least three primary achievements of the organization despite its current status. For a start, it has improved the image of evangelicals in

42. This is, however, a serious challenge that faces every evangelical church in Israel. One of the main accusations that comes from the traditional churches (e.g., Orthodox; Catholic; Oriental; Anglican; Lutheran) is that we are divided into so many groups, sects and streams. This not only applies to the existence of various "denominations," but also to the schisms that occur within individual "denominations" themselves. For example, the single Baptist church established in Nazareth by Southern Baptist missionaries in the 1950s has fractured into six separate churches, all within Nazareth alone!

43. Annual Report 2012, 61–68.

Israel externally. This helps its fulfill its missionary task of reaching out to local Arabs. Secondly, it has also improved the inner-cohesiveness of evangelicals and contributed to the development of a common identity. Finally, the CECI has been accepted as a member of the World Evangelical Alliance (WEA), an international organization that encourages global unity among different evangelical denominations, advocating for their causes and giving them a global voice. Not only does membership increase global awareness of the existence of Arab evangelicals in Israel—a fact that many are not aware of—but it also raises the profile of the CECI in the eyes of the Israeli government by demonstrating that the local churches are part of a unified world-wide body. This will help them when they appeal against the government's decision not to accord them the status of a "recognized community."

Despite these achievements and despite the outstanding goal of attaining official recognition, there are a number of challenges that the CECI will have to face in the future.

For a start, some of the church groups or para-church organizations that are members of the CECI are far better established financially and far better networked with local and foreign organizations than the CECI itself. This might cause a church leader to question the value of continuing to work under the CECI when he or she could achieve more things more quickly on their own. This is a likely scenario given the amount of time required for the CECI to attain such goals as official recognition and unity.

Secondly, as is well known, Israel is a land beset by political and theological controversy with multiple interest groups clamoring to get their voices heard. As an organization representing a number of churches, the CECI has a potential voice and as such is subject to pressure to take a stand on various issues. For example, should it as an organization condemn various Israeli military strikes, should it take a stand on the question of compulsory national service for Arabs, should it become an advocate for social justice issues amongst Israeli-Arabs, or should it have a position on Palestinian statehood? The views of the CECI's members vary on these issues and their common statement of faith alone is arguably too broad to serve as a basis for constructing a consensus.

A third challenge is the fact that almost all the CECI's staff serve in a voluntary capacity. Their work for the CECI is done on top of their other full-time jobs. This limits the CECI's capacity to develop and grow. In recent years the burden this situation imposes has become more obvious, but a lack of adequate funding means that there is no easy solution in sight.

Fourthly, the legal status of an *ʿedah moqeret* potentially stands in tension with the autonomy of the individual denominations and congregations to govern themselves without unwanted interference from the outside. For the time being there is no tension between the denominations (or in case of Congregationalist churches, such as the Brethren, the individual congregations themselves) and the CECI, because the CECI lacks the power (in the form of money, the ability to issue visas, etc.) it would have if it were a "recognized community." Once it does become recognized, however, there is the danger that the executive would use its power to coerce its member congregations to tow the party line. This situation could be exacerbated by the fact that the Israeli government requires a single individual (*rosh ha'edah*) to represent the organization. A weak leader could bow to external pressure from the Israeli government, a strong leader could be abusive and controlling. One possible scenario is that the Israeli government may discover that members of the CECI are evangelizing Jews (a legal though unwanted activity in Israel). They may contact the representative to ask him to stop this activity and then exert pressure upon him if he refuses to do so (for example, by refusing visas to foreign volunteers or building permits for new churches). The CECI will have to develop a system of checks and balances to prevent these developments.

A fifth potential challenge is the issue of guaranteeing adequate representation for each of the member denominations. At the moment, the executive consists of nine members. Five of them must represent each of the five denominations, but a further four are elected. If one denomination, such as the Baptists, should grow in size (they are already the largest denomination), they could dominate the executive and thus heavily influence the direction of the CECI.

Sixth, the exclusiveness of the membership prevents good and respectable evangelical free churches that do not belong to any of the five denominations from joining the CECI. This situation has not yet arisen, but it is a possibility.

Seventh, a significant future challenge for the exclusively Arab CECI is how to negotiate its relationship with the Jewish Messianic congregations. Developing this relationship is imperative to Christian witness in the region. In 2010, the chairman of the CECI sent a warm letter to a national conference (*hakenes ha'artsi*) of Messianic pastors[44] expressing the CECI's

44. We have been informed that there is no official body that represents the Messianic community. This national conference (also called the *klal 'artsi*) is a quarterly meeting

goodwill towards their Jewish brethren in Christ and its desire for further and deeper fellowship. The chairman of the convention responded in kind. Although there is fellowship among evangelical Jews and Arabs, such as a twice-yearly prayer meeting for male pastors and leaders of para-church organizations called "Sitting at Yeshua's Feet," as well as an annual worship event called the Levi Meeting, no further concrete steps have been taken. On the Arab side, one reason is that the CECI is still wrestling with the challenges mentioned above (e.g., the struggle for state recognition; the lack of funding for staff members). Another problem is that the relationship between Messianic Jews and evangelical Arabs is often tense, beset with unresolved theological problems related to the role of the State of Israel in God's plan of salvation, a situation that is exacerbated by the ongoing conflict. On the Jewish side, there may be the issue that in their own struggle for recognition by their Jewish co-citizens as authentically Jewish they do not wish to be seen as advocates for Arab concerns. These tensions have led to an amicable if somewhat distant relationship in which each community is primarily goes about its own concerns (see chapter 5 in this book).

An eighth challenge is the relation of the CECI to the traditional churches (see above). As of yet, the CECI does not have an official position on the matter. There are different approaches among the members, some being more open to building bridges, others rejecting any kind of relationship with them. For their part, the traditional churches have no interest in developing any kind of relationship with evangelicals. On several occasions individual priests have publicly spoken against evangelicals, accusing them of being Jehovah witnesses, Zionists, deceivers, fierce wolves etc. (these statements are not officially sanctioned by the churches but they are not prohibited either [for examples, see §4 in chapter 1 of this book).[45] This has forced the CECI to take a defensive stance, publishing answers to these accusations on evangelical websites without knowing whether these responses reach those responsible for the accusations.[46]

---

of pastors and elders that has no legal or administrative power and in recent years the number of attendees has been dwindling.

45. See, for example, the following two Arabic language videos, one from an Orthodox priest (http://www.linga.org/local-news/MzMyNg) and one from a Catholic (http://www.linga.org/local-news/MzU3Mw).

46. The website Linga, a news portal for Arab evangelicals in Israel, has posted the following two Arabic language responses: http://www.linga.org/local-news/MzU2; http://www.lbc-nazareth.org/ar_news.php?eventid=256.

A ninth issue involves the issuing of certificates for ordination, something the CECI will have to do if it becomes a recognized denomination. Such certificates identify those who are authorized to issue marriage certificates, for example, as well as sign any other official documents. This could lead to tensions within the CECI, however, as different denominations have different standards that their members have to meet in order to become ordained. One possible scenario is that members who are frustrated at not being able to become ordained within a particularly demanding denomination may decide to switch denominations in order to get such a certificate more easily. Another issue is that the board of the CECI would have to submit a list of candidates to the government, which in turn would give the board a certain amount of power over the denominations.

A final potential challenge that I believe may arise is the question of the ongoing significance of the distinctive identity of the various denominations if the CECI as a federation should acquire so much power. This is particularly the case given the small size of the evangelical community in Israel. For example, if a Baptist pastor required a visa for a foreign worker, there would no longer be any need for him to go the Association of Baptist Churches to make an application to the government. He could bypass this organization and go straight to the CECI itself, which would be a far more effective route to take. This might lead to the desire for the CECI itself to become a church denomination in the full sense of the word, planting its own "CECI" churches.

CHAPTER 3

Arab Baptist Leaders in Israel

Their History and Collective Identity

by Azar Ajaj and Duane Alexander Miller

1. INTRODUCTION

This chapter seeks to explore the collective identity of Arab Baptists in Israel. This does not include Baptist missionaries from the non-Arab world or Baptists living in Gaza and the West Bank. Since the Baptist tradition is only about a century old in Israel (see §3 below), and since most of the members of the Baptist churches made a conscious and voluntary decision to become Baptists, we have decided to focus on what is called collective identity. This will assist us in understanding how the community understands itself in relation to other communities.

Tim Green, who has researched evangelical Christians in the context of a Muslim-majority region in South Asia, has offered a helpful model of identity in his study relating the topics of identity, religious conversion, and marriage.[1] Utilizing the model of Benjamin Beit-Hallahmi,[2] he identifies the most profound level of identity as *core identity*,[3] which has also

1. Green, "Identity Issues."
2. Beit-Hallahmi, *Prologomena*.
3. Green, "Identity issues," 439.

been called "ego-identity." This refers to "who I am in my inner self." Since our research is focused on a community and its self-definition, this facet of identity is not our primary interest.

Collective identity should not be confused with *social identity*, however. Social identity relates to "who I am in relation to my group or groups,"[4] or as Syrjänen writes, "*Social identity* is the part of an individual's self-concept which derives from his knowledge of his membership of a social group together with the emotional significance attached to that membership."[5] As different people belong to different social groups (a political party, a tribe, a village, a guild, a particular mosque, etc) so social identity is multifaceted and the claims of the different societies one belongs to may oppose each other. As the identity of an individual changes and develops, it is normal for their core identity and social identity to influence each other.

Finally, there is *collective identity*, which "concerns the way a whole symbolic group is labeled and distinguished from other groups by its identity markers."[6] Collective identity is our main concern here, as we seek to discover how Arab Baptists in Israel have selected certain symbols and identity markers to distinguish themselves from other groups, or alternatively to assert that they are a subset of some larger group. Collective identity is often formulated in terms of affinity/opposition to other communities. In identifying other communities we have chosen a) other evangelicals, b) non-evangelical Christians, c) Jews, d) and Muslims. There are other communities in Israel, like indigenous Armenian Christians, Druze and Baha'i, but these communities are so small and sometimes isolated to one city or area that interaction with them would be very rare and are thus of little significance for our analysis.

Having explained the facet of identity this chapter seeks to explore, we now turn to an explanation of our methodology.

2. METHOD AND RESEARCH QUESTIONS

We identified twenty-two Baptist leaders. Mr. Ajaj, an indigenous Baptist pastor himself, conducted interviews by e-mail, phone, or in person.[7] The

4. Ibid., 440.

5. Syrjänen, *Meaning and Identity*, 57.

6. Green, "Identity issues," 440.

7. If the number of respondents seems small, it is worth pointing out that there are only seventeen Baptist churches in Israel.

interviews took about fifteen to twenty minutes apiece and were all in Arabic. The interviewees were chosen because they are pastors of churches or leaders of other ministries (with student and para-church organizations), and others are lay leaders in their congregations. Of the twenty-two respondents, five are women. This research was conducted in May and June of 2014. The questionnaire used had the following questions:

1. How do you define yourself:
    a. Arab Israeli Christian?
    b. Palestinian Israeli Christian?
    c. Israeli Christian?
    d. Something else
2. A child from your congregation or community tells you that one of his friends at school says he is not Israeli, but Palestinian, another of his friends says he is Israeli *and* Palestinian. He asks you which one is correct and biblical. What do you say?
3. How do you feel when you hear the phrase, "First, we are all Arabs; that some are Muslims and some are Christians is not important." Do you agree or not? Why?
4. How do you feel when you hear the phrase, "Muslims respect and honor Christians, and treat them like equals." Do you agree or not? Why or why not?
5. Do you think it is good to have a dialogue with Muslims? Why or why not?
6. Do you think it is good to have a dialogue with Jews? Why or why not?
7. Do you think it is good to have a dialogue and build relations with traditional churches? Why or why not?
8. What is distinctive about the Baptist faith?
9. Would you preside at the wedding of a Baptist with another evangelical Christian?
10. Would you preside at the wedding of a Baptist with a Messianic Jew?[8] How about a Baptist with a Muslim-background believer?

8. See chapter 6 for more on evangelical-messianic relations.

11. A young woman in your congregation wants to marry an Orthodox Christian man. You know he is a good man and his life is virtuous, and he attends the Orthodox Church. What do you counsel this young woman?
12. Do you prefer to be introduced as a Baptist or an evangelical?
13. What is more important to you when you think about the future of your ministry in Israel: the CECI[9] or the ABC, or are neither important?
14. Is there anything unique about Baptist spirituality that you feel other churches can learn from?
15. What are the main challenges facing Baptists in Israel in the coming years?
16. What are the main positive things that have happened to the Baptist in the last twenty years?
17. What are the major theological issues that addressed Baptists in last twenty years?

These specific questions were chosen with the goal of better understanding how our respondents' perceive their community, both by asking direct questions about their community (such as question eight) and also by using hypothetical but realistic pragmatic situations (such as questions two and eleven). The preference for pragmatic questions over more analytical questions is based on that conviction that "social action is guided by patterned regularities, socially-constructed categories that organize our experience and thinking."[10] It is also important to note that the questions concerning one's relationship to broader communities (Palestinian, Israeli, Arab, Christian/Muslim), as posed in questions 1–4, are actual questions discussed within the Palestinian community and not theoretical constructs.

Before we proceed, it is necessary to provide background information about the Association of Baptist Churches in Israel (ABC) which is mentioned in question thirteen. The CECI is discussed in chapter 2 of this book.

9. See chapter 3 for more information on this topic.

10. Ammerman, "Religious Identities," 212.

4. THE ASSOCIATION OF BAPTIST CHURCHES IN ISRAEL (ABC)

Baptist work was started in the Holy Land in 1911 by a Palestinian from Safed by the name of Shukri Musa (1870–1928). Musa was born into a Catholic family and immigrated to the United States in 1909 due to the difficult economical, social and political situation in the Ottoman Empire at that time. While he was in Dallas, Texas, he was touched be the Baptist teachings and received believer's baptism by George Truett at First Baptist Church in Dallas. After getting his theological training, Musa was ordained and with the support of some Sothern Baptist churches in Illinois he returned as an indigenous missionary to work in the Holy Land. He arrived in 1911, began his ministry in Safed, and later in the same year he moved to Nazareth, where he founded the first Baptist church in the Holy Land.[11]

Additional indigenous leaders were raised up and in the 1920s American missionaries from the Sothern Baptists started to arrive. Baptist Mission in Israel was organized in Israel under the "Baptist Convention in Israel (BCI)," a legal entity which includes all the southern Baptist missionaries and still exists to this day.

Parallel to this American run organization, in 1965 local Arab Baptists also organized themselves under the name "The Association of Baptist Churches (ABC)," with the aim of representing the local Baptists and of working in partnership with the BCI.[12] In the 1990s the International Missionary Board (IMB) of the Southern Baptist Convention in the States changed their policy regarding the goals of their missionary work in the world, deciding to focus all their efforts on reaching unreached people groups rather than continuing to support already established churches. As a result they stopped their financial support to existing Baptist churches in Israel, shifting their focus, for example, to the Druze community, which as of yet has no Christian community. As a consequence, most of local ministries were put under serious financial pressure; this in turn forced some, especially the larger churches, to start becoming self-supporting. Furthermore, the decision caused the ABC to become not merely a fellowship of churches but an important body that is responsible for supporting, encouraging and representing the seventeen Arab Baptist churches in Israel. Beginning around 2000 a new partnership with British Baptists was

11. Watts, *Palestinian Tapestries*, 14–15.

12. Yaffe, "75 Years."

formed and several Baptist associations in the UK became involved in the ministry in Israel.[13]

In chapter 2 an account was given of the CECI, and this section a brief history of the ABC was presented. With that background in place, we are now able to turn to some observations regarding our respondents' answers to our questionnaire.

6. FINDINGS

Most of the Baptists (fifteen out of twenty that answered question one) understand themselves as and identify themselves as Arab Israeli Christians, though some preferred to have "believer" (that is, evangelical) added as well. While some acknowledge the word "Palestinian" as being correct in an ethnic or historical sense, the word is mostly eschewed because it has connotations that appear antagonistic towards the State of Israel, or imply that these people do not wish to be citizens of Israel.

But this view was not universal, as one stated, "We are not Palestinians," whereas another preferred "Palestinian Israeli Christian" over "Arab Israeli Christian." The nuance of this sensitive word comes across in the answer, "We are originally Palestinians but we live in the state of Israel."

Based on responses to question three, we find that there is *a strong preference for a Christian identity* coming before any ethnic or national identity. These people are Christians and this label to them is essential for their self-understanding. In other words, the narrative of pan-Arabism, which advocates the unity of all Arab peoples, often minimizing religious differences, is not influential. One respondent explained, "This might have been true forty years ago when people considered their Arabism more important than their religion. In the last thirty years we find that people are connecting their identity with their religion more than their nationality."[14] One woman reflected that, "It [the statement] has a truth in it, but my values in life come from my faith not nationality."

These Christians do not feel like they are respected by Muslims *as* Christians, though individual Christians may be respected as being trustworthy or influential. This is further evidence that the pan-Arab conviction is dead among Baptist leaders. Some mentioned recent events in Syria,

13. Mansour, "A Brief Summary."

14. See chapter 1 for similar developments among traditional Christians in the West Bank.

Egypt and Iraq as evidence that many Muslims are antagonistic towards Christians. Our respondents do not appear to agree with the Western conviction that Islam (correctly practiced) is peaceful and tolerant.

In relation to our questions about *religious dialogue* (questions five and six), there is a general embrace of it with Muslims and Jews, but this is explicitly tied to a desire to see Muslims and Jews consider the possibility of becoming disciples of Jesus Christ. This is a different vision of religious dialogue than what is common in the USA and Europe, where religious dialogue generally precludes a desire for religious conversion. A couple even said that dialogue was not worthwhile, and that evangelism was the appropriate course of action.

Regarding *ecumenical relations* with the traditional (and generally more powerful) churches of the Holy Land (question 7), there was near-unanimity that this is a worthwhile and valuable endeavor. But this conversation (which is only just now in an embryonic phase) should not try to paper over genuine doctrinal and liturgical differences that clearly exist. This represents an important change in attitude, as formerly an ecumenical dialogue with these churches was seen in a negative light. We believe that this shift in perspective is related to the reality that thirty or forty years ago almost all Baptists had recently converted from these forms of Christianity (especially the Greek Orthodox, Greek Catholic and, to a lesser degree, Roman Catholic). If so, this would appear to represent a process of maturation leading to a self-awareness that Baptists in Israel define themselves less according to who they are not (Orthodox), but rather focus on who they are (evangelicals). One respondent wrote, "Yes, this is even more important than the others [dialogue with Jews and Muslims], especially because the historical tension between us could come out of not knowing each other very well."

On the other hand, most respondents would not approve of the wedding of a Baptist with a Christian from a traditional church (even if he/she is observant and devout; see question twelve). However, a Baptist marrying another evangelical was not objectionable to anyone. This was the case even with a believer who came from a Jewish or Muslim background, though there were concerns about different cultural expectations within these communities. This appears to mean that Baptists center their identity around a particular doctrinal tradition (held in common with Messianics and ex-Muslim Christians) more than certain cultural customs (which are held by Arab Christians from the traditional churches).[15] It is worth noting that with one exception (a pastor's daughter marrying a Messianic Jew), the case of marriage with a Messianic Jew or convert from Islam was hypothetical.

Question eight asked, "What is *distinctive about the Baptist faith*?" A number of "distinctives" were mentioned. Some felt that the Baptist faith was *reasonable (mantaqi)*, which probably is meant to distinguish it from some "superstitions" in other religions and forms of Christianity, and also from the "emotionalism" of some forms of charismatic Christianity. There was also an appreciation for the Baptist tradition of endorsing freedom of religion and freedom of conscience for all people. Several respondents mentioned "order" (*tandhiim/nidhaam*). This appears to be related to the fact that the ABC has a new constitution and experiences orderly transfers of power, elections and decision-making regarding the ordination of new pastors. Furthermore, when controversies arise these issues are preferably dealt with by committees (though this does not always happen, as will be seen below in relation to church splits). An example of this is the ordination committee, which was formed as a subcommittee of the ministry committee in the late 2000s. If this interpretation is correct then it represents an instance of these Arab Christians valuing and endorsing aspects of church government learned from American and British Baptists. Other answers referred to preaching and teaching that applied to people's daily lives in a simple and "biblical" manner.

Question twelve was asked in order to reveal if there is a strong preference for one communal title over another—Baptist v. evangelical. During the interviews most respondents were hesitant to give a clear answer, understanding the labels as more or less interchangeable. In the end the division was more or less half going each way. This appears to mean that the specific label "Baptist" in the public arena is not foundational for Baptist communal identity.

When asked about the *main positive changes* (question sixteen) that have taken place in the last twenty years, the main three things listed were the founding of Nazareth Evangelical Theological Seminary (NETS; see

15. The number of Messianic Jews in Israel is estimated by local evangelicals at around five thousand, though there is no way to verify this number. Miller has previously estimated the number of Muslim-background believers in Israel at around three hundred. (See Miller, *Living among the Breakage*, 295) For more on the thorny issue of conversion from Islam to Christianity in Israel see Ajaj, "Baptism and the Muslim Convert."

chapter 4 in this book),[16] the addition of new leaders, and an openness to teachings about the Holy Spirit.

The foundation of NETS in 2007 and the decision to accommodate charismatic Christians within the ABC both represent instances of agency (the exercise of power) in developing their own identity. The seminary was identified as important because, while some of its faculty is foreign, it offers indigenous scholars the option to study divinity, Scripture and theology in a manner that, while influenced by English and American curricula, is also intentionally aimed at addressing pastoral and theological issues of special importance to Christians is Israel. Furthermore, the seminary's library and research programs allow for Christians in Israel to engage in research and writing related to issues like the Israeli occupation of the West Bank and Gaza, Christian witness to Muslims, the difficult issue of Zionism in its many varieties, and so on (see chapter 4 of this book).[17]

Closely related to the seminary is another factor that several respondents mentioned, which is the entry of a new generation of leaders. The relation to the seminary is clear, as many of them have studied or are studying at NETS, and have thus both formed the spirit and ethos of the seminary while also being formed by the instruction offered there, specifically the graduate-level Bachelor of Divinity program offered in conjunction with Spurgeon's College Online and the Arabic-language Bachelor in Theology degree. The seminary's relations with international educational institutions like the Asian Theological Association, Spurgeon's College (London), and Hope International University (California) provide students and faculty the opportunity to be voices for evangelical Arab Christians in Israel. Other students have been trained at Galilee Bible College (GBC), an initiative of Bethlehem Bible College.

In relation to communal identity the seminary represents a step towards autonomy and self-rule for the ABC, meaning that it can now accomplish the important goal of obtaining accredited degrees for local Christians, while also allowing them to be educated and formed within their own cultural matrix. That the ABC founded an evangelical but not explicitly Baptist seminary is also noteworthy, for it shows their openness to other denominations within the evangelical tradition.

16. Both authors of this paper are on the faculty of NETS.

17. For more on the founding of NETS, which was originally called the Nazareth Centre for Christian Studies, see Association of Baptist Churches, "The Nazareth Centre."

But what is meant by "greater openness to the Holy Spirit," cited by numerous respondents as a key change? Beginning in the 1990s, partially encouraged by a veteran Southern Baptist missionary from the USA, the ABC allowed for charismatic Christians and congregations to join the ABC, though the official theology of the Association never became charismatic. This represents a departure from the theology of the International Missionary Board (IMB, the missionary sending body of the Southern Baptist Convention in the States), which holds that gifts like tongues and prophecy had ceased at the formation of the New Testament Canon (ironically, the missionary who encouraged this development belonged to the IMB).

Other answers referred to the growth in number of churches and the centennial celebration of Baptists in Israel, which took place in 2011.[18]

In relation to *key challenges* facing Baptists, the most-mentioned topic was official state recognition which is outlined in the chapter on the CECI (chapter 2). Two other key challenges were mentioned by numerous respondents. These were church splits, and finances. The problem of finances appears to be related to the decision of the Southern Baptists from the USA to discontinue financial support for Baptists in Israel, which was mentioned above.

The issue of church splits is related to the common reality that divisions among leaders often result in one leader taking a group of his friends and family and leaving a particular Baptist church in order to go and found a new one. All but one of the Baptist churches in Nazareth, for instance, started this way. While the respondents noted their appreciation for the order and constitution of the ABC, this serves as a reminder that not all divisions and issues are being handled through these avenues.

Other key challenges mentioned by a few people were related to maintaining a Baptist identity in the context of such a small number of Baptists and the formation of the CECI (see chapter 2), encouraging the role of women in ministry (which does not mean ordaining women), and the challenge of speaking clearly on political issues.

7. CONCLUSION

Communal identity is centered on the conviction that humans belong to certain groups or communities to differing degrees. Moreover, those communities—Arabs, Israelis, evangelicals, Baptists—have complex and

18. For more on the Centenniel see Reynolds, "Baptists in Israel."

dynamic relations to each other. We wish to explicitly recognize the limitations of the scope of this study on Baptist identity in Israel. The interviewees were not chosen at random, are more male than female, and are all leaders (or former leaders). As such, this study represents a snapshot of how certain leaders of the rather tiny community of Baptists in Israel think about themselves in relation to others—other evangelicals, other Christians, Jews and Muslims. Notwithstanding these limitations, though, we can present the following findings, recommended for further testing by other researchers:

Not only is this community led by indigenous leaders, it in the process of contextualization. "In the earlier part of the twentieth century, Protestant missionaries had tended to use the term 'indigenization' to describe their aim of establishing churches which should be authentically indigenous in governance, financial viability, and ownership of their own mission . . ."[19] The ABC is clearly indigenous (though still partnering with foreign missionaries, when needed), but contextualization represents the next step beyond simply being self-governed. Baptists in Israel are engaged in a process of contextualization. Contextualization, as defined by Shoki Coe, represents a "double wrestle" (his term), as a community wrestles with God's world, which is to say their own contextuality, and with God's Word, meaning Scripture and their own Christian heritage.[20] In Coe's thought, this represents the next step after indigenization, which meant the transfer of leadership to indigenous agents. In doing this the Baptists have identified some aspects of their own (imported) heritage which they cherish, like church governance, while also identifying certain things to leave behind, like the cessationist doctrine[21] which they had received from some American Baptists.

Moreover, this process of contextualization is ongoing today, as the Baptists (within the context of the CECI) struggle to obtain official recognition as a religious body (and not simply as a series of non-profit groups) from the State of Israel. The foundation of the seminary in Nazareth is also good example whereby the local Baptists identified a need (local

19. Stanley, "Inculturation," 22.

20. Coe, "In Search of Renewal" and "Theological Education."

21. That is, the doctrine that teaches that certain of the gifts of the Holy Spirit, like speaking in tongues or prophecy or miraculous healing, ceased to exist upon the completion of the writing of the books of the New Testament.

theological education and well-educated leaders) and then went about making it happen.

Second, Baptists in Israel appear to build their identity primarily around evangelical doctrinal commitments. That is to say, being Baptist is interpreted as one of various ways of being evangelical. The primacy of the evangelical facet of identity can be seen in unproblematic acceptance of marriage among different forms of evangelicals, and even the (mostly hypothetical) willingness to see an evangelical married with a Messianic Jew (whose doctrinal commitments are largely evangelical) or an Muslim convert to evangelical Christianity, while having grave reservations about an evangelical marrying a non-evangelical Christian.

Third, their identity is centered on their Christian faith, much more than their nationality (being Israelis) or ethnic origins (as Palestinians/ Arabs). That many respondents specified that they are a Christian first, and only then Arab or Israeli is evidence for this.

Fourth, there is a conviction that at the heart of their relation to Muslims and Jews is the traditional evangelical belief that evangelism must be first and foremost. Those who favored dialogue did so with the specification that this would allow for relationships to be formed wherein one's faith might be shared. The trope, so popular among some in the West, that Islam is tolerant and peaceful is nowhere to be found.

Finally, Arab Baptists in Israel appear to be fairly apolitical.[22] When asked about future challenges none mentioned that more political activism against the occupation of the West Bank was needed. This should not, we think, be read as indifference to the difficulties of life under occupation, but rather as an acknowledgement that such activism is not likely to be effective or yield any benefit.

But after concluding with these observations it is important to remember that ". . . religious identities are neither simple nor uncontested but need active construction and interpretation."[23]

Two specific areas emerged in this research as loci for possible future activity. These are dialogue with the traditional churches, and a concern for the problem of churches splitting. Will the Arab Baptists in Israel take up the challenge of trying to formulate a concrete way of responding to these issues? Or will they simply acknowledge that they are important issues

22. For examples of politically active Protestants in Israel-Palestine, see chapter 1 above and Kuruvilla, *Radical Christianity*.

23. Jørgensen, *Jesus Imandars*, 415.

while not in fact exercising agency to address them?[24] The questions are presented to future researchers and also to our respondents.

24. An example of an indigenous response to church splits is the ongoing doctoral work by Rula Mansour, who is analyzing the nature of these splits from a sociological perspective and seeking theological avenues by which to address the problem.

CHAPTER 4

Nazareth Evangelical Theological Seminary

The First Six Years

by Azar Ajaj

ALMOST EIGHT YEARS HAVE passed since I, Azar Ajaj, received an email from Bryson Arthur inviting me to work with him; he had been asked by the Association of Baptist Churches in Israel (ABCI) to found a theological institute in Nazareth. Over the years I have not only been an eyewitness to the establishment of Nazareth Evangelical Theological Seminary (NETS), but also deeply involved, with Bryson and others, in founding and developing this seminary into a place for preparing and equipping evangelical Arab leaders for this country. Therefore, on the occasion of Bryson's decision to depart from Israel and go to work in Jordan Evangelical Theological Seminary in Jordan (2013) I have decided to write this recollection in order to share the story of NETS and the significant role Bryson has played in the life of our seminary.

1. HISTORICAL BACKGROUND: EVANGELICALS IN THE HOLY LAND

Free Church evangelicalism in the Holy Land goes back about a hundred years. Various denominations were able to establish congregations in Nazareth, Haifa, Jerusalem, Acre and Jaffa during the British Mandate.

Unfortunately, many of these churches were left nearly vacant as a result of the 1948 war. At that time, many Arabs, including evangelicals, fled the conflict and became refugees in neighboring countries like Lebanon, Syria and Jordan. A good number of leaders left at that time too; therefore, churches needed to reestablish themselves from almost nothing after the establishment of the State of Israel.

Different evangelical missions started to organize their work in the new state, and one of the major concerns was training indigenous pastors and leaders. These leaders, they hoped, would be able to revive and carry on the work that had been decimated. Baptists in Israel were pioneers in this area, and for the next thirty years or so, after 1948, several Arab pastors were sent to Baptist seminaries in the United States or the Baptist Theological Seminary in Ruschlikon, Switzerland.[1] In addition to that, a Bible school was opened in Haifa in the 1960s. It functioned part-time and intermittently until the 1990s. While several leaders and lay people took part in the programs and courses, no one managed to complete a degree at this institution.

The Church of the Nazarene also used seminaries and training centers to educate their pastors and leaders. Their college in Cyprus, East Mediterranean Nazarene Bible College (which was moved to Jordan after the peace agreement with Israel in 1994), was their base for training leaders in the Middle East through intensive courses offered during the summer. The Nazarene European College in Switzerland also provided training for pastors and leaders. The Assemblies of God founded the Galilee Bible College in Haifa from late 1990s, and it continued to serve the local community until the early 2000s. Many of those currently pastoring with the Assemblies of God (and other churches) received their theological training in this college.[2] Bethlehem Bible College (BBC) was another institution where several pastors and leaders received training and degrees, whether by studying at the main campus in Bethlehem, or at the extension in Galilee which helped a good number of leaders to complete degrees begun at other institutions.[3]

1. Such as Fuad Sachnini, the pastor of Evangelical Baptist Church in Nazareth; Philip Saed, pastor of Haifa Baptist Church; the late Suhail Ramadan, pastor of Tur'an Baptist Church; George Kazuora, pastor of Rama Baptist Church; Zahi Naaser, who pastored Acre Baptist Church for a short period (later he left the Baptist denomination and joined the Anglican Church).

2. Such as Marwan Beem, Yousef Dakwar, Victor Bahbah, Jamil Wahhab, Soheil Dabbagh, Maroun El Raheb, Ehab Ashkar, Albir Saliba.

3. I should note that I received my first degree from BBC.

In the end, however, all of these shut down except the Galilee extension of BBC. There were a number of reasons for this: sometimes funding dried up, sometimes courses were offered only sporadically, and some places offered only one or two courses a semester (meaning that it would take many years to complete the program). The Galilee extension of the BBC continued to offer courses, but there were Christian leaders (especially in the ABCI) who desired a local institution based in the Galilee which would be relevant to the needs and challenges of the Christians in Israel.[4]

Through all of these years what was missing in the country was a theological institution that was based in the area and which could serve the evangelical community in Israel in particular, and the wider Christian community in general.[5] Such a place would assist future pastors and leaders to receive training and to be equipped for the ministry without leaving the country, with substantial savings on costs, of course. This need became more pressing with the growth of the evangelical churches, both in size and number as well as the aging of several pastors who were nearing retirement. Finally, the increasing number of educated members in the churches led pastors to acknowledge the need not only to receive training, but also to receive a proper degree which would make them more compatible with their members.

2. THE EARLY INITIATIVES

So far, I have summarized the reality which evangelicals faced when it came to the issue of training their pastors up until the year 2000. However, the beginning of the new millennium witnessed movement on this issue and new hopes appeared on the horizon. In the year 2001, Bryson and May Arthur came to Israel commissioned by the Church of Scotland, after spending six years in Kenya where Bryson had lectured in systematic theology. They began work at Mar Elias University in the village of I'billin.[6] Bryson's main

4. For the reader not familiar with Israel-Palestine, it is important to understand that the Galilee is in Israel, and the Arab Christians from there are Israeli citizens, whereas Arab Christians in Bethlehem do not have Israeli citizenship and their ability to travel is very limited.

5. I'm focusing on Arab-led local ministries and that is why I'm not discussing other valid local institutions.

6. This University was founded by the Greek Catholic Bishop Elias Shakour, author of the well-known book, *Blood Brothers*.

task was to establish a theological department at the university.[7] Soon after they arrived in Israel, they started attending Local Baptist Church (LBC) in Nazareth, the congregation which they joined as members a few years later. The relationship with the church helped Bryson to build ties with other Baptist churches, as well as the ABCI. This had positive implications for his ministry at that time and in the future.

In a year or so, as the head of the theology department at Mar Elias, Bryson was able to bring together a group of lecturers and started the first class shortly after that. Although Mar Elias is a Catholic institution, about ten Baptist students joined the class.[8] Two factors stand out here. First, Bryson's good reputation among the Baptists (as just indicated above) helped to assure potential Baptist students of the balance and quality of the program. Second, we have here an indication of how eager these Baptist students were to get theological training, even at an institution that is not evangelical.

In 2003, due to a financial crisis in the Church of Scotland, several of their missionaries around the world had to return home. This was the case for Bryson and May; they returned to Scotland where Bryson served as an interim pastor, and May went back to work in midwifery. But prior to returning to Scotland Bryson was approached by the then-chairman of the Association of Baptist Churches in Israel (ABCI), Fuad Haddad, and the Secretary, Bader Mansour. They asked him to explore the possibility of starting an evangelical college. Bryson expressed his willingness to start such a college and even worked on preparing a curriculum. However, at that time the ABCI faced the major challenge of the lack of facilities for the project, which was therefore postponed.

3. THE ESTABLISHMENT OF NETS

For almost a period of two years the ABCI had been negotiating with the Southern Baptist International Mission Board (IMB) to acquire the "mission house" in Nazareth. This house had been built in the 1950s to house the main Southern Baptist missionary to Israel and given that the IMB had pulled out its missionaries from this field it was selling the property. The ABCI's goal was to use it as an administrative center and as a Bible college

7. "Mar Elias Offers Higher Diploma in Theology," www.comeandsee.com/view.php?sid=263.

8. I was one of these ten students.

as well.[9] Though an outright donation was not on the table, the IMB did offer the ABCI a 25 percent discount on the purchase price. The ABCI agreed to the offer, and in June 2005 the house was purchased[10] with the help of two generous gifts, one from Dr. Dwight Baker (a Sothern Baptist missionary who had lived in the house), and the other from two donors from the US, Wayne and Buena Stevenson.[11] The road had been paved to go ahead with original plans of founding a new college.

The invitation to Bryson and May to return to Israel was extended shortly after that. Bryson often tells the story as follows: "One day I had a call from Bader Mansour, who said, 'With a very great struggle we have bought the building. Will you come to head up a Christian college?' My answer was definitely yes. Even without asking May."[12] With great excitement and delight, in May 2006 Bryson and May came back to Israel, this time to live in Nazareth. A few months after their return they went to Kelsey Language Institute in Jordan, where they took an intensive course in Arabic for four months. Then Bryson and I and others from the ABCI started the hard work of preparation, and on September 2007 the Nazareth Center for Christian Studies (as it was originally named) was officially opened. The ABCI website gives a report about this opening as follows:

> Monday the twenty-fourth of September 2007 marked the official opening day of the Nazareth Center for Christian Studies in Israel. The day was the much anticipated end result of months of patience, prayer and hard work. To celebrate the occasion, a ribbon cutting ceremony and special dedication service were held on the newly acquired grounds, featuring several distinguished speakers. Highlighted among these speakers was David Coffey, the current leader of the Baptist World Alliance.[13]

Bryson's leadership and ministry commenced mainly upon their return from Jordan, when he worked to build a team of faculty and staff, form a vision, sort out the academic programs, and raise the funds needed. We now turn to a summary of those tasks.

9. Ireland, "Israeli Baptist."

10. Mansour, "The Nazareth Center."

11. "Dr. Dwight Baker," 12.

12. I relate the story as I have often heard it told.

13. "Baptist World Alliance Leader Speaks at Opening of Nazareth Center for Christian Studies," http://www.baptist.org.il/news/post/1.

3.1 Vision

The original name that was given to the seminary was "Nazareth Center for Christian Studies." This name was changed to Nazareth Evangelical Theological Seminary (NETS), a name which the faculty felt communicates better the purpose and vocation of the institution. However, the vision of NETS that Bryson and the steering committee had (see next point) from the very beginning had not changed:

> To advance, equip, and inspire, from an evangelical perspective, the Christian community in Israel through profound theological and biblical training and reflection, effective leadership training, and promoting reconciliation and unity within the body of Christ.

These three points in the vision—theological training, leadership training, and reconciliation—became the three pillars for the vision of the NETS ministry and shaped the different programs that were offered.

3.2 Management

On the 27th of February, 2007, a steering committee was formed. The members of the committee were: Bryson Arthur, Director of NETS; Bader Mansour, Chairman of the Steering Committee; Azar Ajaj, Finance Officer; Philip Hill and Peter Eyre[14] (Brent Neely, from the Assemblies of God, joined later). The Steering Committee functioned for almost two years and later on it was replaced by two committees: a management committee and a board. As time went on, officers and members were added to both. As for administration, May Arthur has had a great number of responsibilities during the past seven years. She was assisted by Angela Hill (wife of Phil Hill) and others from time to time.

3.3 Faculty

The faculty started with four lecturers: Bryson Arthur, Brent Neely, Azar Ajaj, Lisa Loden (former director of Caspari Center) and the librarian, Maye Ashkar. In less than a year the number of the faculty members grew to seven, when Alex Miller (of the Episcopal Diocese of West Texas), Phil

14. Both from Central Baptist Association in the UK, and were involved in establishing a partnership with the ABCI churches since the year 2000.

Hill (his ministry with NETS was through Unevangelised Fields Mission or UFM), and Scott Bridger (then serving with the Baptist Convention in Israel [Southern Baptists]) joined NETS. In 2009 Makram Misherki (a member of the Exclusive Brethren denomination) also started to teach at NETS.

3.4 Academic Programs

In September 2007 NETS opened its doors to local students, offering the Bachelor of Divinity degree through the open degree program of Spurgeon's College in London. A partnership providing for the MTh degree with International Baptist Theological Seminary (in Prague) also was established later. However, only one class with three students joined this program, and it was replaced later with an MA in Ministry degree in 2011 (in conjunction with Hope International University, Southern California). As outlined in the vision mentioned above, in addition to these degrees NETS also sought to provide significant leadership courses through the leadership department led by Lisa Loden. The Ministerial Formation sessions led by Phil Hill helped the students to apply what they had learned to their various ministries and was a source of encouragement for many.

All of the above programs are of high quality, yet a serious challenge with them was the English medium required for student papers and assignments. Even though substantial help with English was provided by May and others, this was no remedy for those who have no English at all. Therefore, an Arab language degree was needed. This became possible after the partnership that Bryson established with Program for Theological Education by Extension (PTEE) in Jordan (2009). At that point, students with no English were able to do a fully accredited degree (BTh) taught in their first language.

Another task Bryson and the NETS faculty set themselves was to help students and leaders from abroad to better understand issues that are relevant to our context, issues such as Islam, Eastern Christianity, and Judaism. To this end the NETS team worked to offer courses for international students and Christian leaders from around the world. These programs are offered through intensive courses for students from the USA and through a sabbatical program. During these intensive courses students and visitors receive lectures, many of them at the historical sites of the Bible themselves—the ruins of Caesarea, the shores of the Galilee, or one of the many sites around Jerusalem.

A Certificate of Christian Studies was also designed by May Arthur and Alex Miller to train Sudanese students who were refugees in Israel from 2006 to 2012. This unaccredited degree had to be offered in English to students who had, in many cases, a very irregular and challenging educational background. It was clear that the seminary would not earn money by providing classes for refugees, but the Faculty Committee decided that offering this training was integral to the seminary's mission. Most of these refugees were deported back to their country, and some of these former NETS students are leading churches there presently.

A similar program is also offered for Filipino foreign workers who are members of the Filipino Baptist Church in Tel Aviv. The aim of this training is to help them to minister while they are working in Israel.

To summarize, we can say that in a relatively short time Bryson was able to found a good theological institution, a seminary which seeks to impact the lives of indigenous Christians within the country, as well as believers from further afield. Preserving a balance between indigenous and foreign staff permitted the seminary to grow in a healthy way and helped it to communicate both with Westerners and locals.

4. A TIME OF TRANSITION

As we read in the book of Ecclesiastes 3:1: "To everything there is a season, and a time to every purpose under the heaven." As the seminary matured, some of the board members focused on increasing the visibility of the indigenous Christians at the seminary. As mentioned, the seminary launched the BTh in Arabic in 2009, and it became clear that offering degrees taught in Arabic was vital. For this reason and others, Bryson and May felt that the college needed to be headed by a local Christian. At around the same time, Bryson was offered the position of academic dean at a larger seminary, the Jordan Evangelical Theological Seminary (JETS). And so, in August of 2013, they left Israel for Amman.

Presently the seminary is facing both challenges and opportunities. In terms of challenges, our leadership is changing. Phil Hill, who was our director of ministerial formation, accepted a position at Wales Evangelical Theological Seminary and left Nazareth in June of 2013. Alex Miller, the seminary's academic dean departed in October of the same year, returning to the USA to teach and minister in San Antonio, Texas. There are also ongoing talks between the ABCI and BBC, exploring how NETS and the BBC extension in the Galilee might work more closely together in the future, perhaps ultimately even merging to form a new institution. After Bryson's departure in June, I was appointed president of the seminary; I continue to work with Brent Neely, our seminary vice president, and our faculty and staff as we as carry out our vision.[15]

5. A VISION FOR THE FUTURE

As I think about how to carry out that vision as a seminary, I want to focus on the following three points: first, we hope to develop and create our own theological degree programs taught in Arabic. Second, we have recently added pastor Abu Ghazaleh (originally from Jordan) to run our ministerial formation program. One of his main ministries is to mentor ordinands and recently-ordained ministers. Third, evangelical Christians in Israel, while still a small community, have reached the point of maturity were we can and should do our own research; I envision NETS as a center of lively research which will serve the church, both locally and globally.

Returning to the occasion of this paper, I want to underline the fact that Bryson will be remembered not only as one who started a ministry very well, but also as one who finished his ministry well. His encouragement and support to his team are an example to others, especially in this area of the world where leaders in general tend to accrue benefits and privileges for themselves. Also, May's diligent work, whether in administration or in the English language support she gave to so many students, will be remembered always.

15. Since writing this article much progress has been made. The merger has been included and a new institution has been created with the name Nazareth Evangelical College (NEC). Brent Neely has returned to the states and the faculty is currently entirely Arab.

CHAPTER 5

Yearning for Unity

How Evangelical Arabs in Israel View Messianic Jews

by Azar Ajaj

ALMOST THIRTY YEARS AGO I received my first invitation to attend a training seminar held by the Fellowship of Christian Students in Israel.[1] I had just finished high school at the time and was getting ready to go to university. This was not only the first time I had taken part in any kind of student activity, it was also my first opportunity to discover that there were also Jews who believed Jesus was God's promised Messiah! This was a great surprise; it was like suddenly discovering that I had brothers and sisters I had never known about. *Hallelujah*! With the naivety of a young believer I thought to myself, "Here is the solution to the conflict of this country: the solution is called the 'body of Christ.'"

For me, however, this was not a merely romantic idea. Since that time I have become, directly and indirectly, involved with different ministries and activities where Arab and Jewish believers work together. It has been a great privilege to work side by side with several Messianic brothers and sisters. However, during this time I have also come to realize (and this is not an insight unique to myself) that this unity I had dreamed of is not yet within easy reach.

1. For the official website, go here: http://old.fcsi.ws/.

Despite this, my original dream has not evaporated. Rather, it has become my deep conviction that the Body of Messiah (Arabs and Jews) is the only hope for the conflict we are living in and that mutual love and respect between these ethnically distinct believers should be the model of divine peace in this land. This is what motivated me to do research on how evangelical Israeli Arab leaders (pastors, youth leaders and leaders of para-church ministries that serve among Israeli Arabs) view their relationship with Messianic Jews. Do they think this relationship is important? Are there any obstacles that hinder it? What is the best way forward?

Before I outline this research, I should briefly explain why I decided to focus on Christian Arab citizens of Israel alone and not Christian Palestinians in general: first, although Israeli Arabs are ethnically Palestinian (we refer to the inhabitants of the West Bank and Gaza as our "Palestinian brothers"), the challenges we face are different. Israeli Arabs do not face problems with occupation, walls, or restrictions of movement. We do have arguments with the government on certain issues, but these arguments are aimed at helping the Israeli Arab community in general, and the Christian one in particular, to better integrate with Israeli society and to claim full rights as citizens. This is to say that in order for the Arabic-speaking church in Israel to be relevant to her own people, she must deal with theological and social issues distinct to those faced by the church in Palestine. Second, as far as relationships with Messianic Jews in Israel are concerned, Israeli Arabs are trying to go beyond the issue of "reconciliation" in order to ask how we can function and work together as the Body of Christ for the sake of this country, providing a rare example of coexistence in a land where such cooperation is rare.[2]

I hope and pray that this presentation of what Arab pastors and leaders think on this issue will help create a framework in which sincere people from both sides can continue their dialogue. Some of this will be hard to read, since raw feelings and emotions will be expressed. However, there can be no hope of progress, change, or truly Christian relationships without communication that is based on openness, honesty, and truth.[3]

2. This kind of unity has become even more difficult between Messianics and Palestinian evangelicals due to the restrictions on travel and the Separation Barrier erected during the Second Intifada. Currently, Israeli Jews are forbidden by the Israeli government for security reasons from entering areas under Palestinian control.

3. For similar sentiments from the Messianic Jewish side, see Aaron Abrahamson's thoughtful comments on his experience at the *Lausanne Initiative for Reconciliation in Israel/Palestine* (LIRIP), in which he describes the "gruelling work" of reconciliation that "initially

RESEARCH QUESTIONS AND METHODOLOGY

The life of a minority that wishes to preserve its identity and agency is generally challenging. A small subgroup must either swim upstream or submit to the majority. However, as an Arabic poem puts it: "God might turn the curse to a blessing." In my research, the fact that the number of Arab evangelical pastors and leaders in Israel is so small actually worked to my advantage, since it allowed me to meet and interview most of them personally concerning their relationship with their Jewish brothers and sisters (I met with thirty-four altogether, which represents about 90 percent of the Arab evangelical leaders in Israel). The decision to focus this research on evangelicals only is due to the fact that Messianics are, for the most part, evangelicals themselves, and so the shared common ground creates greater potential for unity. Many traditional Arab Christians (Catholic, Orthodox, Syriac, etc.) consider all evangelicals to be heretics, whether Arab or not.

The pastors and leaders I interviewed belong to one of the five evangelical denominations in Israel (Baptists, Assemblies of God, Closed Brethren, Open Brethren and the Church of the Nazarene) and several para-church groups in Israel.[4] The interviews were held between July 2012–February 2013. All the interviews were arranged ahead of time, with a clear explanation of the purpose of the research. While I gave the interviewees the option of not answering any given question, none of the questions were left unanswered.[5] The aim of the questions was to discover whether Israeli

opens up more wounds than it heals" (http://www.faithstreet.com/onfaith/2015/02/24/messianic-jews-palestinian-christians-and-a-theology-of-reconciliation/36244).

4. With the exception of the Closed Brethren, these denominations have been united in the Convention of Evangelical Churchs in Israel (CECI, simply called the *majma'* in Arabic).

5. The questions are as follows: 1. The age of the person; 2.The place of their Theological training; 3. Do you believe that the state of Israel is a fulfillment of Old Testament and New Testament prophecies? Explain. 4. Do you believe that there is a special role for the Jews in the End Times? Have you ever changed your position on this and if so, why? 5. Do you think that the issue of the End Times is an obstacle for the relation between the Arab Christians and Messianic Jews? 6. Do you teach/preach about this subject in your church? Or do you avoid it since it is difficult and causes disagreements? 7. Do you think that differing theological views among Arabs have a negative effect on relations among Arabs? 8. Have you ever invited a Messianic speaker to your church to preach? How many times? Have you been invited to a Messianic congregation to preach? 9. Do you believe it is important to build relations with Jewish believers? If so, what helps the building of these relations? 10. Do you participate in programs with Messianic Jews? If so, give some examples. 11. Do you believe that Arab Christians should play any kind of

Arab leaders believe that relationships with their Messianic brothers are important or not, and if so, what challenges and barriers exist and what can be done to overcome them. Given that I would like the results of this research to aid mutual understanding, it was necessary to ask questions concerning what Arabs think about "the others," in particular how they feel about typical beliefs and attitudes held by Messianic Jews on such sensitive topics as the relation of the State of Israel to the Old Testament and God's ongoing plans, to the role of the Jews in the divine economy, and so forth.[6] In order to have a healthy relationship, we need to be open and transparent and, with humility, let our partners know what we think about them, even though articulating these views in public can be painful and awkward. By revealing what these evangelical leaders think about these issues, problems are revealed and the way is opened to finding solutions. Regardless of the truth value of the various opinions expressed in the interviews, I believe these responses can help to form a basis for a healthy dialogue between leaders from both sides who seek to strengthen the relationships.[7]

I the first section of this article I summarize what the interviewees felt were the main challenges to the relationship. I then look at their suggestions for making progress. The reader can take this data as it stands and formulate his or her own conclusions. The presentation of this data is then followed by my own analysis. I hope this provides the reader with some sense of direction for the future and the possibilities that lie ahead of us.

EVANGELICAL ARAB ISRAELI VIEWS OF ISRAELI MESSIANIC JEWS

All but two of the interviewees expressed his/her[8] deep conviction that the relationship between the two groups is extremely important, since this relationship is vital to expressing the unity of the Body of Christ in this country (The two interviewees who did not prioritize this concern did so out of

role (spiritual, social, political) in relation to the Israeli/Palestinian conflict? If yes, what is this role?

6. It seems to me that Arab leaders relation to Messianics as a single group, even though there is diversity within the group.

7. It should be pointed out that these leaders know me personally and so felt safe expressing their views as they trust me.

8. In the Arab world, it is still extremely rare for women to have positions of leadership. For this reason, most of my interviewees were male.

practical and not theological reasons). Nevertheless, they also stated that the current state of this relationship is not as it should be. In their opinion, several factors have contributed to either lukewarm or non-existent relationships. The factors can be summarized as follows: the issue of the land, the Messianics' commitment to their Jewish identity, the political situation, cultural differences, historical events, low prioritization of the relationship, and the influence of foreign Christians. We shall now look at their views on each of these issues in turn.

Land and State in the Divine Economy

The most common major challenge mentioned by most of the interviewees (twenty-six out of thirty-four) was the emphasis that Messianics place on the teaching that the creation of the State of Israel is the fulfillment of prophecy and that it has a significant role to play in end time events. It is important to note here that the issue with this is not the theological belief itself. Arab evangelicals do not have a united position on this. Sixteen of my interviewees believe that the creation of the State of Israel is the fulfillment of prophecy, eleven do not believe so, and seven of them have no position. Despite these differences, most of them (twenty-seven interviewees) expressed their resentment at the injustice done by Israel to the Palestinians whereas only two of them believe that a Palestinian country would contradict prophecy. The rest do not see any problem at all with the establishment of such a country in the West Bank and Gaza. Furthermore, nine of the interviewees think that this issue forms a barrier among Arab Evangelicals themselves.

The issue for my interviewees is the way this belief has become so central in the theology of many Messianic Jews, so much so that any other eschatological position is taken to be a simple contradiction of the Word of God. Furthermore, many feel that acceptance of this eschatological position is made a condition of fellowship.

A few interviewees added that the exaggerated centrality of this theological position is aggravated by the fact that Messianic Jews also often draw political consequences from it, often tending towards the right wing of the political spectrum.[9] For a few of my interviewees, this is the main factor

9. For example, during Israel's military offensive on the Gaza Strip in 2007, the Messianic Jewish convention *Haqenes Haartsi* published a two-page endorsement of the war in the Jerusalem Post, a move many Arabs felt was one-sided and inconsiderate to the

determining the depth of the relationship between Messianics and their Arab brothers and sisters. Some strong statements were presented here by a number of leaders. For example:

> The issue for me here is not what they believe theologically but the way they apply their theological convictions when dealing with Palestinians. Does the fact that the State of Israel is a fulfillment of prophecy mean that there is no place for the Palestinian nation here? Is she (Israel) immune to criticism and so has the right to humiliate the Palestinians? Should we as believers rejoice in this?

Another leader emphasized the inequality in the approach to this issue between the two groups:

> You would find that most of the Christian Arabs have a great sympathy with their Jewish brothers and sisters and understand the difficulties they face from their own people [i.e., that they are accused of not being "Jewish"]. They even understand their position concerning the issue of the land. Yet the Jewish side does not manifest the same level of understanding. It is true that in various aspects they share a similar faith with the Christian Arabs, however this shared faith disappears when it comes to the issue of the land and the State of Israel. There is no understanding directed towards a people who have their own story (the Palestinians), a story which the Messianics do not like to hear; there is no sympathy for a nation, much of which was expelled from its own land and lost its freedom to live in dignity. This story is not over, and the wounds are still open.
>
> I feel very sad when I find that my Jewish brothers value the land more than the human being. And despite their faith in Christ and their love for their Arab neighbors, it seems they might love them more if they would leave the country, since this place is meant to be only for the Jews.

Others are convinced that Messianic Jews' positions on the issue of the Land are totally political and not theological at all and that the problem exists because they have turned this political stance into a major doctrine in their congregations. One leader concludes, "They have become prejudiced in this position to the point that we cannot separate them from the racist and unjust politics of the country."

---

suffering of their people in Gaza.

The Jewish People in the Divine Economy

Related to the issue above is the question of the ongoing role of ethnic Jews in God's plan of salvation, for most Messianics believe that they have a distinct role to play within the church that is not shared by Gentile Christians. This was held to be problematic by almost half of my interviewees (seventeen out of thirty-four). Again, the issue is not *necessarily* a belief in an ongoing role for ethnic Israel. As with views concerning the state and prophecy, opinions vary on this (for example, twelve interviewees believe that God has a distinct role for the believing Jews; it is also worth noting that some of the leaders who believe the state is the fulfillment of prophecy do not connect that conviction with Jewish believers in any special way). The primary issue is the way this belief leads Messianics to separate themselves from their Arab brethren, for example by celebrating the Jewish religious holidays and not the Christian ones, refusing to be called "Christians," refusing to join or mix with non-Messianic normal churches, and so forth.

Some strong examples may be quoted here: "The fact that they believe that they are the nation elected by God makes them look down on us, the Arab believers. This allows our relationship to grow only to a certain point and it stops there." Or, "Their pride prevents a good relationship between us and them. They are still God's people according to their understanding to the Old Testament, and beyond that they also have discovered the Messiah; so all this adds to their status." Some even take it more seriously and feel that this attitude is more than arrogance but becomes a form of racism: "This fact turns some of them to identify themselves as Jews before anything else, and in some cases they even become racist." To summarize, half the Arab leaders feel that although all are one body in Christ, they still feel that the Messianics consider themselves better than the gentile believers.

Political Tensions

Most of the pastors who mentioned the political obstacle to healthy relationships between the two communities were aware that both groups share responsibility for allowing this problem to interfere.

The political situation is very tense in the Middle East in general and in Israel in particular. This increases the tendency to polarization between the two groups as both seek to be accepted by "their own people." This can be seen in the political positions adopted. Many of my interviewees felt that

Messianic Jews had a tendency to be more right wing, perhaps even seeking to stress their Jewishness more than their Messianicness. This is true also for the Arab Christians when they seek to be part of their own people and allow the frustration and discrimination that Arabs in Israel experience dictate the way Arab Christians think and behave. For example, it was said by several pastors that they are afraid to be classified as "Zionists" and traitors by other Arabs if they publicly acknowledging their religious and spiritual connection to their Jewish brethren. As a result, they, too, are very careful when it comes to relating to their Jewish brothers and sisters.

Cultural Differences

The interviewees observed that both communities come from different cultures and languages, with different ways of dealing with life and that this inevitably leads to difficulties in relating to one another. Many of my interviewees admit that they are not making enough effort to encourage their members to build bonds with their Jewish brothers and sisters.

Historical Background

This issue was highlighted by only two pastors, but it is worth mentioning since it deals with our identity as Arabs. According to one interviewee, one of the reasons for the weak relationships is the "victim mentality" that Arabs have that prevents them from establishing a right relationship with "the nation that has been the reason for their suffering." On the other hand, they feel they usually are the ones who are expected to compromise and make sacrifices: for example, in any joint meetings, they need to sing, share, and communicate in Hebrew; to be accepted by the international Christian community and by the Messianics they need to believe what others expect them to believe. All of this builds a wall, a "separation barrier," in their hearts and minds. These pastors indicated that, ironically, "We are in fact pleased with this barrier. We are here and they are there; it is safer and less of a headache" (this is a citation of one pastor who was consciously alluding to the separation barrier between Israel and the West Bank as well as the slogan of the former Israeli prime minister Ehud Barak, who said that the barrier was good because it kept them there and us here).

Lack of Prioritization

According to seven interviewees, part of the distance between the two communities was related to a lack of good communication between the two groups, and this on two levels:

1. First, we don't spend time together, do not talk to each other, and therefore, we reap what we sow.
2. Second we do not communicate the importance of this relationship to our congregations.

As a result we are raising a whole generation without motivating and encouraging them to develop or value a relationship with their Jewish brothers and sisters.

Different Treatment by Other Christians

Despite the fact that Messianics are not themselves responsible for the following factor, the different treatment by other Christians was mentioned by several leaders as a source of tension. The interviewees claim that Christians around the world favor the Jews and their ministries in Israel even though Arab Christians are an integral part of the Body of Christ in this land. They often feel that they are ignored or forgotten. This favoritism appears on two different levels:

1. The first one is awareness: evangelical Arabs claim that Christians in the West make efforts to be acquainted with and involved in what is happening with the Jewish believers and their ministries, yet there is very little effort made to learn about the Arab Christians in Israel. In fact, according to the interviewees, many Christians around the world do not know that such a group even exists.
2. The second form of favoritism is related to financial support. Arab churches are small and most of them are not self-sustaining. Therefore many pastors and leaders struggle financially and wonder why only the Jewish part of the body of Christ is cared for by Christians abroad. They wonder, "Are Arab Christians somehow inferior, or Jews somehow more important?"

SUGGESTIONS FOR BUILDING ONE BODY

Having outlined the obstacles and challenges as perceived by my interviewees, it is easy to become pessimistic about the prospects of fostering positive and fruitful relationships between the two communities. However, these concerns come from people who also have ideas about how to improve the relationship. For instance, only two interviewees said they did not care much about relations with Messianic Jews (One did not feel that this is contributes anything to his ministry, the other believed that all the relationships with the Jews are artificial and not real, therefore we do not need those relationships). All the rest expressed their conviction about the importance of this matter. Statements included: "Extremely important, since we are one body." Or as one said, "We are not allowed *not* to seek to build this relationship." With that in mind, we will now turn to some of the interviewees' suggestions for improving the Messianic-Arab Christian relationship.

Ministering Together

Ministering together is the best way to bring us closer. One of the interviewees described this as similar to what we find in the book of Nehemiah, where all people were involved in doing something together. This was repeated in one way or another by most of the leaders, who made several suggestions:

- Joint prayer meetings
- Participating in outreach campaigns together
- Fellowship meetings between the two groups (which should be frequent and not connected only to a season or an event)
- Having conferences, trips and study days together
- Joint youth work
- Exchanging pulpits

The Issue of Land and State

In relation to recommendations for improved relationships, seventeen leaders mentioned the land. With respect to how this issue can be part of the solution, the responses can be divided into two groups.

Nine do not believe in or encourage any open and frank talks about the theology of the Land and prophecies that might be related to Israel. The reason for this position was the feeling that such a dialogue will not only not have good results, but will probably harm relations even further. The relationships are already tense, and the way to improve them is through conversations about basic beliefs common to both groups. We ought not focus on the secondary or political issues. However, if for any reason this issue must be discussed, then let it happen with small groups of people who are mature enough not to let this subject damage their relationships.

The other eight people had exactly the opposite point of view. They strongly believe that it is important to speak openly, frankly, and directly about differences of opinion regarding the theology of the land and the question of whether the State of Israel is a fulfillment of prophecy or not. There is a need to face the challenge this issue brings to the communities and so we should not avoid it, even though it is a thorny issue. Our Jewish brothers and sisters should hear our story, one leader said, and they should hear what happened to our people, our land, and our villages. This is not in order to make them feel guilty, but to help them understand the gravity and sensitivity of this subject for Arab Christians.

Listening to Each Other

This matter was mentioned by eleven leaders. Although it might appear that it is related to the previous point, the concept of mutual listening has a wider implication because it refers to listening to each other *in general*, and not solely on the issue of the land and state. My interviewees expressed their desire to have a relationship built on knowing the other and allowing the other to know them. When this happens, it will be possible to pray for each other in a genuine way, to be part of the other's ministry, and to serve and care for each other. The issue here was not "how to do it" but rather to acknowledge the importance of this mutual listening and the willingness to do it.

Unconditional Acceptance

Finally, while listening to the Arab leaders I could strongly sense their desire to build healthy relationships with Messianics but also their resistance to any pre-conditions, whether theological or political, that might be placed on such relationships. Consider the following statement:

> We should accept each other despite our different positions on different issues, as long as Christ is the center of our relationship, and should focus on the role of the Body of Christ before anything else. The differences in our opinions should not divide us, and we can have unity in spite of our diversity. This only can happen when we decide to accept each other in Christ.

INTERACTING WITH THE FINDINGS

So far I have simply presented the responses of the interviewees without providing any interaction from my side. The situation we are talking about is complex and very delicate, but some of the statements made above cry out for analysis and additional reflection. Therefore, the following section will interact with the information gathered from the interviews and analyze it, in the hope that some helpful conclusions can be drawn.

Theology and Politics

I will start with the most controversial issue, namely the State of Israel (and the related eschatology) and its role in fomenting tension between the two groups. The issue here is not primarily different theological or even political positions but rather *how* the Messianic Jews apply this theology in their daily practice. Eschatology and the different interpretations of whether the State of Israel is a fulfillment of prophecy or not are subjects that are not dealt with in most of the Arab Evangelical churches (neither do most churches teach or preach about Palestinians having their own state). Only four pastors said that they teach about this in their churches and *all* of them emphasized that it is not a central subject. Their main task, regardless of their positions on Israel, is to bring the Good News to the people around them, leaving the other issues to God. As a result of this Arab evangelical approach, two problems appear when the relationships with Messianic Jews are on the table.

First, because the Arab evangelicals marginalize this issue in their ministry and teaching, they are surprised or disappointed when Messianic Jews do not do the same thing. According to Arab evangelical theology and practice, this is a secondary issue and should not play any role in determining their relationships with the Messianics. We hear this clearly in statements like, "We should focus on the central subjects in our relations," and, "we should accept each other as brothers and sisters in Christ, with no previous conditions." Therefore, there is a difference in priority here: for Arab evangelicals this is a secondary issue, while—from the perspective of my interviewees—for many Messianic Jews it is a primary issue. What is called for, then, is a meta-discussion, or a conversation about conversations—why is this matter more important to one group than to the other?

Second, in the opinion of twenty-four Arab leaders, many Messianics offer unconditional support to Israel and its policies, or they are simply silent when it comes to issues like injustice towards Arabs. This puts the evangelical Arab leaders in an awkward position and forces them into a corner in their relationship with broader Christian Arab society. On one hand, they value the relationship with their Jewish brothers and sisters, on the other hand, they must be careful not to compromise their ministry to Arabs, many of whom feel oppressed and aggrieved by Israel. Often the traditional churches will label evangelical Arabs as Zionists, due to the prominence of Christian Zionists within the Western evangelical stream. A strong, visible relationship with the Messianics might provide fodder for the local critiques of the Arab evangelicals.

Interestingly, when I asked about suggestions to enhance the relationships, only eight of the twenty-four leaders who believe this is a major challenge, thought that this was an issue that they should personally address. This was a somewhat confusing result: why do many of them believe that Israel and eschatology is one of the major obstacles to unity, and yet they categorically do not want tackle it? Three possibilities might be suggested here.

1. First, since most of the leaders believed that joint ministries, fellowship, praying together, etc., will strengthen relations, it is possible that they hope that by doing such things it will be easier to deal with the theological issues later.

2. Second, it also could simply be an Arab cultural factor of preserving honor or stability by avoiding confrontation. That is, by avoiding confrontation they hope to maintain a "good" relationship.
3. The third possibility is the conviction that conversations about this issue will not bear fruit, perhaps largely based on frustrating prior attempts. On the contrary, it might complicate the relations between the two groups even more.

The Minority Factor

Arab evangelicals in Israel are a small minority. In fact, it is more accurate to say that they are a minority within a minority within a minority. As Arabs, they form 20 percent of the whole population of Israel. As Christians they constitute only 10 percent of the Arabs in Israel, numbering around 160,000 individuals.[10] As evangelicals, the number is no more than five thousand.[11] On each one of these levels, evangelical Arabs are faced with a number of different challenges. As Arabs, they must often struggle to achieve equal rights with their Jewish co-citizens. As Christians, there is a fear of oppression from Islam, especially with the rise of intolerant, radical Islamic political movements in the Middle East and in Israel. As evangelicals they can be subjected to verbal attacks from the traditional churches, who often associate them with Zionists (as mentioned above), Jehovah's Witnesses, and various other movements deemed subversive or dubious.

All these different forms of pressure play a major role in shaping the mentality and the behavior of evangelical Arabs. In relation to this research, I can see this happening in two areas. First, although the evangelical Arabs are a very small minority, they are aware that they belong to a larger evangelical family around the world.[12] However, they find it disappointing when they feel that their family is not aware of their existence; it is more frustrating when they find that at the same time this family is fully aware of, involved with, and supportive of their brothers who live in the same land.

10. Central Bureau of Statistics: http://www.cbs.gov.il/reader/newhodaot/hodaa_template.html?hodaa=201211349.

11. There is no official number for evangelicals, this is an estimated number. This estimate based on my knowledge of these churches.

12. For instance, most Arab evangelicals belong to a denomination (Baptists, Assemblies of God, Nazarene, etc.) that is a member of the Evangelical Alliance of Israel, which itself is a member of the World Evangelical Alliance.

Some might call this "jealousy." I do not think that the word "jealousy" is the right word here. I believe that it resembles rather the sense of being "abandoned" or "forgotten." However, even if I am mistaken, what is important is the fact that these feelings of being neglected result in bitterness and distance towards the Messianics.

Second, at each of these levels evangelical Arabs are expected to compromise in order to please the majority. As Arabs there is a general expectation within Israel that they should grateful for the benefits that the Israeli state has brought them—often with comparisons made to the different conditions in surrounding Arab nations. They are also under a lot of pressure to constantly prove to the Jewish majority that they are not terrorists or committed to destroying the state. When they criticize Israeli policies, they are often accused of being traitors to the nation. As Christians they try to avoid any problems or confrontations with Muslims due to the fear of violent responses; often, this is the only way they can live in peace. As evangelicals they always need to prove their legitimacy to the traditional churches. I am not claiming here that they never go against the majority; they *do* from time to time. However, these expectations are the reality they have to face.

When it comes to relationships with their Messianic brothers and sisters, they also find they are expected to compromise. In order to receive the right hand of fellowship, they need to adjust their eschatology to the "orthodox" (dispensationalist) one. Since this relationship is an optional one (unlike their connections to the state, Muslims, and the traditional churches), many evangelical Arabs prefer to minimize their interaction with the Messianics. Among other things, this is a way to avoid both compromise and confrontation.

Lack of Initiative

Although the suggestions of ministering together sound good, it was not clear who would be responsible for coordinating such activities. Most of the interviewees who suggested this spoke about it in the third person, meaning they hope that "someone" will originate, organize, and fund such programs. Not a single interviewee took the responsibility upon himself or outlined how he personally could contribute to such an effort. To my knowledge, even when many of these leaders had the opportunity for fellowship with Messianics through joint programs and conferences, they did not develop these into deeper connections. As an example of the relative lack of initiative, only a few of the leaders have ever been invited to speak in a Messianic congregation, and even fewer of them have invited a Messianic Jew to speak in his church.

A main reason for this attitude might be the issue of priorities. Yes, the relationship with the Messianics is important, but there are other important issues in the ministry of these leaders that demand their time and effort. Therefore, they are willing to take part in different mixed activities coordinated by others, yet they are not interested, or do not have the time, to invest in or initiate anything themselves.

CONCLUSION: SOME PERSONAL REFLECTIONS

Any serious relationship requires commitment, transparency, investment and sacrifice. This certainly applies to the relationship between Messianic Jews and evangelical Arabs. In my opinion this relationship is not an optional one: our role and responsibility as the body of Christ, especially in this country, is to reflect the peace and unity we have in him. Was this not Jesus' desire and prayer in John 17:11, namely that we "may be one"? And is not our love to each other a direct command from him? This love, which can be seen by others, is the sign that we are Jesus' disciples (John 13:34–35).[13] This does not require good will only, but also true commitment. If the interviewees were sincere (and I believe they were) when they expressed their desire to have a closer relationship, then this requires reflection, prayer, teaching, and preaching about the importance of this relationship. It will also need an intentional effort to find ways to build and strengthen the bonds.

Certainly, I agree that we should be sensitive to our own people, but this should not be an excuse to hide behind. We should seek to communicate our challenges and the concerns we have with our Jewish brothers and sisters. Leaders have to open their hearts and share with love and care about things that create this breach between the two. One cannot have a healthy relationship while harboring something in his heart against the other person. Otherwise, we will be building a house on sand which will fall down when the storms blow. There is risk in any relationship, but if we believe in

13. Of course this does not apply only to the relations between these two groups. Evangelical Arabs should seek to have this within their own community, and the Messianic Jews should seek the same as well.

its worth and value it and are convinced it is God's will, is it not appropriate to be ready to pay the price? If Arab pastors and leaders truly value this tie to their fellow Jewish followers of Christ, they cannot maintain this relationship only behind the scenes. An example of this dilemma from a biblical and Jewish context is found in the pages of the New Testament: Peter believed that the door of the church was open for the gentiles; he had fellowship with them; and yet, he behaved differently when he felt pressure from fellow Jewish Christians (Gal 2:11–12). This is not the leadership model we should aspire to, and Paul was right to rebuke Peter for practicing it.

Finally, if we are calling on Jewish believers to understand and accept us, are we aware that this is a double-edged sword? Do we realize that we also need to open our ears and hearts and try to understand and accept them without setting preconditions? In fact, we should do that whether or not it is reciprocated. We are called to respond to God's word and not the behavior of others. Today is the day to do the right thing. Moreover, it would be very good if a Messianic brother or sister would take the initiative and do a similar study among the Messianics. This might also help the evangelical Arabs to better understand their Messianic brothers and sisters. It could help to build a platform where both engage in a healthy dialogue that will contribute to building the kingdom of God in this country.

CHAPTER 6

Christians from a Muslim Background in Israel and the West Bank

by Duane Alexander Miller

A DEFINING FEATURE OF the evangelical movement is its commitment to evangelism, the communication of the Gospel to non-believers with the hope that those who hear it will believe and convert. Within Christianity at large, this commitment is not unique to evangelicalism, but it is a central feature of evangelical identity. In the context of the Middle East, where Muslim conversion to Christianity is so fraught with danger, this strong emphasis has meant that it is evangelical Christianity rather than more traditional Christianity that has either led to the conversion of Muslims or been the context in which the new faith is nurtured. The particular context of these CMBs (Christians from a Muslim Background) along with their challenges and relations to the various churches is the subject of the following chapter. It is both based on first hand fieldwork in the region and set in the context of the broader Middle East.

1. THE STATUS OF THE APOSTATE IN THE WEST BANK AND ISRAEL

Since CMBs largely end up attending evangelical churches, and since it is largely evangelical Christians that evangelize and/or catechize these believers, this chapter will be concerned with religious freedom. It focuses on the sensitive but important question of religious conversion from Islam to Christianity: freedom for the Christian community to present their message to Muslims and, if that message is embraced, to accept that new member into their community; and freedom of the Muslim-background individual to engage in religious conversion, which is to say turning from Islam (or aspects of Islam) and turning to Jesus and his religion, which is, in our context, understood to be Christianity, and his followers, which here means, in some sense of the word, the church.[1]

In general these Muslim-background believers are seeking conversion and initiation, but have not been baptized and do not belong to a local gathering of Christians. They do have the interior conviction and experience of having turned away from the old of Islam and to the new of Jesus and the faith he and his followers taught, though. It is perhaps most accurate to consider such individuals (and they are often isolated and alone) as marginal believers. Their theology tends to be evangelical or charismatic, for those are the communities that are most engaged in presenting the Christian message to Muslims, but they do not often belong to a local evangelical denomination, be it Baptist, Assemblies of God, Brethren or something else. In spite of this, the tendencies and spirituality of these CMBs tends to be strongly influenced by an evangelical ethos for the reasons outlined above.

In order to better understand the difficulties faced by CMBs we must examine their context in greater detail. In relation to the established churches, their presence is either hidden or (more often) not acknowledged at all. In Israel, Muslims have the freedom of religion and conscience to leave Islam for another religion or no religion at all. In the West Bank this is disputed. In Hamas-controlled Gaza this would likely lead to execution, which according to Al Bukhari *jihad*, 149, is the explicit punishment levied by the Prophet for people who leave Islam. There exists unanimity among the four schools of Sunni jurisprudence regarding the matter dating back to the first century AH, though there is disagreement regarding the fate of the female woman apostate—some preferring imprisonment until return to Islam over execution—and the question of whether the apostate should be offered a chance to recant or not.[2] The words of the Prophet on the mat-

1. The nuance is needed because there exist allegations (but to date, no falsifiable evidence) of communities that have turned to the message of Jesus enunciated in the Bible without having left the Islamic society and culture. These alleged movements are called "insider movements."

2. Ahmed An-Na'im, "The Islamic Law of Apostasy."

ter appear unequivocally clear: "*man baddala diinahu fa'aqtaluuhu*—who so changes his religion, slay him."[3]

There were differing opinions among the Christians I interviewed in Jerusalem and the West Bank on the matter. I therefore visited a (Muslim) lawyer in Bethlehem who kindly answered my questions (free of charge) about religious conversion: "Can people change religions here? I mean, from Christian to Muslim, or Muslim to Christian?" I asked, trying to make the question non-threatening. His answer, in impeccable classical Arabic which could only be mustered by a jurist or poet was, "Your answer comes in two lines: the Christian may become a Muslim, but the Muslim may not become a Christian." When asked why, he explained that the Palestinian Constitution specified shari'a as a source of law, and this was the opinion of the shari'a on the matter. He specified that the legal bases for this were found in the hadiths of the Prophet. Many of the Christians we interviewed, and ex-Muslim Christians as well, were clearly aware of this. In Palestine this sentence might well be carried out (though not by the PA), as it was in the case of Ahmad al Achwal, though only after he was allegedly tortured in the prisons of the PA,[4] or they might be expelled from their homeland because of their Christian faith. Such individuals are relatively powerless and can therefore make few demands for justice, whereas traditional, orthodox Islamic justice specifies execution for them. Even if the state turns a blind eye to their apostasy, their family may well take matters into their own hands.

2. HOW CHURCHES AND SOCIETY INTERACT WITH CONVERTS FROM ISLAM

2.1 In the West Bank

The focus of this book is on evangelical Christians, but for the sake of integrity and comparison, I also investigated the question, what would the Catholics or Orthodox do if approached by a person who wanted to convert? This is an important question here because an explanation of why

3. Some Islamic scholars, like Ahmed Subhy Mansour, have called into question the validity of the hadith. For this he was labeled a *kaafir* and was forced to flee from Egypt to the USA. See his *The Penalty of Apostasy*.

4. As related in Weiner, *Human Rights of Christians*. In fact, the book was dedicated to him.

converts do not join the traditional churches is an important aspect of their context.

Various answers were presented. One was that conversion could indeed take place if done quietly and away from the public eye (though this does not mean the government will legally recognize the validity of said conversion). Other respondents felt that this would sow sectarian discord, endangering the discourse of the one Palestinian people wherein religion is secondary to nationalism. In other words, the presence of the convert implies something that can be found in Christianity but that cannot be found in Islam. This could hurt the feelings of some Muslims and lead to discord. Thus the freedom of the Muslim to leave Islam and the freedom of the church to welcome the convert were seen as less valuable than that of sustaining united Palestinian-ness. In the West Bank, this was the response we most often heard: that the potential convert should be turned away (or sent to some other church) because welcoming in converts is too dangerous or risky.

Another response involved welcoming the convert from Islam in secret, so as to prevent sectarian divides and potential violence. While not completely surrendering the freedoms involved, this approach represents concealment of those freedoms for the sake of maintaining civil order and security. One Palestinian convert[5] I met told me of her search for a church that would accept her. She had read some Christian material and had become convinced of the truth of the Christian faith. One local priest allowed her to attend church but would not baptize her and eventually tired of her insistence for baptism. Another priest (from a different church) gave her a key for the church building so she could come and pray on her own, but said that he could not baptize her. An old monk I met in Jerusalem (neither Catholic nor Greek Orthodox) told me he could help her. I asked, would you baptize her? He said no, he couldn't. And I asked if his bishop would (many churches only allow bishops to baptize adult converts). He said, no, that his bishop would never do that. But, he said, he knew an old, retired priest who would do it, though the baptism would take place in a bathtub, with me as sponsor, and in secret. (This course of events did not come to pass, though she was eventually baptized.)

With few exceptions the churches in the West Bank do not appear to feel their right to welcome converts from Islam is an important one. Or, if it

5. Here and throughout some minor details have been changed regarding the converts in order to ensure their security.

is important, it is not worth the repercussions that will come along with it. Converts are few and far between, and publicly welcoming a single convert could, they seem to think, lead to violence or punishment. Moreover, as some said explicitly, converts from Islam will be killed. Thus one person in the West Bank said, "We have freedom of religion here, but not like in the West, where a person can change their religion." Another Christian (not ex-Muslim) in Bethlehem explained that while her (Protestant) organization was devoted to liberation and freedom, they would not accept a person who wanted to convert to Christianity from Islam. Ironically, some representatives of the traditional churches, who by and large expressed a derogatory view of evangelicals, who are not recognized by the PA or the State of Israel, said that when they get a Muslim asking about Christianity they send them to the evangelicals, who are, it appears, the community that might at least answer a Muslim's questions.

My conclusion is that for the seeker or secret convert who is seeking baptism or instruction in the Christian faith, outside of the local evangelical communities—if indeed there are any—there are very few avenues available. This study of context helps reveal at least one reason for why it is that CMBs are largely evangelical in their theology and spirituality in the West Bank.

2.2 In Israel

In Israel, the situation is different. Muslims in Israel have the freedom to convert, and Christians in Israel have the freedom to openly incorporate Muslim converts into their churches. I estimate that there are about three hundred or so CMBs in Israel, and perhaps a few hundred more in the West Bank. Nonetheless, this rarely happens. In Israel, persecution will not originate from the state, but according to a Catholic priest in Jerusalem (where, independent of the occupation, citizens are under Israeli law) they can welcome Muslim converts, but they will often be persecuted and even killed by their families.

3. THE CHALLENGES AND INTERESTS OF THE CHRISTIAN CONVERT FROM ISLAM

3.1 Belonging and Community

Freedom as a concept is closely tied to interests, for the free person is able to pursue their interests. And so turning to the interests of the CMBs themselves, they are various. One of the key challenges they face is the local church, as intimated above. Because of this, some CMBs do not attend Arab churches, but prefer to attend Hebrew-speaking home congregations made of mostly of Messianic Jews. Messianic Jews, who believe that Jesus of Nazareth was indeed God's messiah, are not generally accepted by the larger Jewish population as genuine Jews. As such, they are liminal or marginal figures. CMBs are too—the Muslim community does not accept them because of their apostasy, the Arab Christians do not accept them because of suspicion, a (perceived) long history of abuse at the hands of Muslims (though this is only spoken of in private), their precarious situation as a tiny minority, and their desire to not harm the "one people" discourse. One congregation in Israel that I visited was both Arabophone and also openly welcomed CMBs and Muslim enquirers, but this is the exception. The converts who attend a Messianic home church demonstrated creative agency in relation to belonging and assembly. In relation to freedom, we are speaking of freedom to belong to a community larger than one's self, after one has been expelled from their original family and community. Agency was exercised here on various levels to preserve freedom of assembly, or more precisely, freedom of community or even freedom to belong.

During an interview with a Protestant cleric in Israel, he related how he had baptized a couple of Muslims (and Jews) over the years. After thorough catechesis and making sure they understood what they were doing, and that their motives were sincere, he would baptize them, submit the documents to the State of Israel for change of religion, and then register them not with the local Arab congregation, but an international (and thus largely expat) one in a large city. These people could avoid the rejection of Arab Christians while also legally belonging to a recognized church, and as such they had the legal rights of belonging to that established church in Israel, which meant that issues related to inheritance and burial and marriage would be handled by Christians, not Muslims (see chapter 2 for more details; this option would presumably not exist in the West Bank). The CMBs who attended an informal home church of mostly Messianic Jews did not have these rights, as their congregation is not recognized by the state, but they did at least have the possibility to belong to a community of people like them—liminal, rejected figures.

The difficulties related to community and belonging may lead one to pose a further question: why do these liminal CMBs not simply form their own churches? The answer is that, in the larger framework of the Arabophone world, they have done just that. Almost all of the Christians in Algeria belong to such communities. Also, a case study exists of how one such group came into being, rather accidentally, though the specific location cannot be disclosed.[6] In most places, though, they do not exist in sufficient numbers to form such churches, and also, one claim of the Christian faith is that it "breaks down the wall of hostility" (Eph 2:14) between different communities, and so CMBs (many of whom have read the Bible quite rigorously) are justified in seeking to be incorporated into a heterogeneous and variegated community.

3.2 The Challenge of Employment

If employed by a Muslim then the apostate will likely lose their job, and if their landlord is Muslim, they will likely lose their place of residence. These things are especially true in the West Bank where there is little legal recourse for the apostate. I knew one young man, a convert in the West Bank, who moved to a new city and started to work for a Christian man at his store. When the storeowner learned that he was a convert, he fired him. If he had been born into a Christian family there would have been no problem, but it was simply too dangerous for him to have a convert working for him.

In Israel proper, there is less likelihood that one will be fired for converting. If someone works for a family-owned business it could happen. But if one works for the government or a larger company, then as long as a person continues to do his or her work in a manner that is not disruptive, they should be able to continue with their work.

The reality of discrimination in relation to the freedom to work has made churches in other parts of the Arab world focus on offering training and job skills so that the convert will be able to start their own businesses,

6. Chapter 4 of Miller, *Living among the Breakage* (the abstract and PDF of this PhD dissertation are available at the author's blog: http://duanemiller.wordpress.com/2013/04/29/contextual-theology-making-and-ex-muslim-christians-abstract/.

though I am not aware of any such initiatives in Israel-Palestine. From the point of view of the few Christians who will relate to converts from Islam, there is a desire to avoid the creation of dependency by giving the convert money or long-term employment. The concern here is two-fold. First, doing this may attract insincere converts, thinking that conversion means employment; and second, that these ministries or missionaries often have very limited funds and simply cannot afford to do this.

3.3 Converts as Sources of Pollution

Apostates from Islam have crossed a boundary that, it is thought, endangers the safety and cohesion of the entire community. As such, they are treated as a polluting presence that must be contained, eliminated or purged.[7]

Therefore, a key difficulty faced by ex-Muslims is related to family dynamics. As a Lutheran in Bethlehem explained to me, the question of religion is wrapped up in family identity. There exists the conviction that leaving Islam necessarily means betraying one's family, and alienation from family is widespread among CMBs. Even if Muslim family-members want to continue to relate to a convert, there is often overwhelming social pressure to force/entice the convert to "return to Islam," or to rid the region of the polluting presence of the apostate. There are various strategies for achieving that, including keeping the convert confined, killing the convert (which is rare, but does happen), forcing the convert to emigrate (more common), or forcing the convert to quietism (also common).

All of these strategies for containing or eliminating the polluting presence of the ex-Muslim involve circumscribing their freedoms, though this is much more pronounced in the West Bank than in Israel. The first strategy involves removing their freedoms of movement and assembly by more or less imprisoning them in their family's home. The second involves the loss of all freedoms. The third, exile, involves robbing someone of the freedom to live in his or her homeland. Ironically, Palestinians often speak of being forced out of their homes as a great injustice, while in fact this is a regular way among Palestinian Muslims of dealing with Christians who converted from Islam. The final form of dealing with pollution is to allow for the person to remain but make sure that their polluting message does not spread. This represents an agreement not to speak about Jesus or the

7. The concept of pollution used here is largely influenced by Douglas, *Purity and Danger*.

Christian message, and probably an agreement not to attend a local Christian congregation.

The ex-Muslim Christian community in Israel-Palestine only numbers in the hundreds, though it has grown substantially in the last two decades. How are these Christians working to promote their own freedom? The community in Israel-Palestine in itself is so small and young that it is hard to say with any precision how agency is being exercised on more than an individual scale. On a larger scale, when we examine the writings (mostly autobiographies focusing on their religious conversion) of ex-Muslim Christians, including those from countries like Egypt, Iran and Pakistan, it is possible to identify some clear instances of agency in relation to freedom in particular.

4. AGENCY

In spite of these difficulties, CMBs do appear to be working toward a number of goals, one of which is the subversion of unjust social structures.[8] The unjust structure which is targeted as being inhumane and unjust is nothing other than the Islamic shari'a itself, for it is the shari'a that prohibits them from enjoying their freedom to live in their home, to work where they like, to have their religious conversion acknowledged by the state (as in Egypt, Jordan and Palestine, though not in Israel, Turkey or Pakistan), to assemble with fellow Christians in safety, to share their views on religious matters in safety, and so on. One response to all of this is to explain that the shari'a is in fact very diverse and dynamic and there are theories of it that allow for religious conversion and tolerance. Such an objection is pointless though, because that is not their lived experience of shari'a. The shari'a they know is the one lived out in their societies, not the contemporary, more liberal forms found at American and British universities. CMBs in their writings advocate for freedom of religion, including the freedom to leave Islam for another religion or no religion at all, and that such a decision should be acknowledged officially by the state where the state keeps track of such things; freedom of speech, including speech that is critical of Muhammad and the Qur'an and what are often perceived as misogynistic Islamic customs; free-

8. As argued in Miller, *Living among the Breakage*, chapter 5, this means that we can speak of this as a form of liberation theology. This, however, should not to be confused with the "Palestinian Liberation theology" of Naim Ateek, who does not endorse the conversion of Muslims to Christianity, as he told me in an interview.

dom of assembly, in relation to being able to meet and worship with fellow Christians in safety; freedom in relation to family law, in that converts should be free to raise their children in a Christian household, and that marriage and burial should be handled according to Christian guidelines for the convert and not according to the shari'a.

Returning specifically to Israel-Palestine, though, we do not find a community that has either the will or the security to engage in such practices. In Palestine they experience persecution on multiple levels, and the state has no interest in providing security for them, and may well have an interest in facilitating those who wish to delimit their polluting presence. Many of the Christians in the West Bank are keenly aware that apostates are to be killed, and told us that in no uncertain terms. Churches stand little to gain in terms of welcoming in converts from Islam, and have much to lose. Thus, converts or seekers are either turned away, received in secret but without initiation (baptism) and visible incorporation in the Christian community, or referred to the few (mostly evangelical) churches that might interact with them.

In Israel, churches are not endangered to the same extent by welcoming in CMBs. Much depends on who controls the police force in a given region or city though. If the local police force is Arab, then it is almost certainly Muslim (as is the case in Nazareth), and it is unlikely that vandalism of churches will be punished. If the police force is Jewish, I don't know. Also relevant is the visibility of the violence. Mere vandalism will probably not be punished, but burning a church or killing a convert—that violence reaches a level of visibility that might shame the police forces into securing some level of justice for the Christian.

In general, though, demanding justice and safety for CMBs is not considered to be in anyone's interest. And so, of all Christian populations in Israel-Palestine, this is the most powerless and abject one. Their experience reports that Islam is unjust and oppressive, an opinion that would make many people uncomfortable. Their mere existence seems to imply that Islam, properly understood and practiced, is neither peaceful nor tolerant. If nothing else, these converts do have freedom of conscience, and it is precisely this freedom that they have exercised in leaving Islam for Christianity

5. MOTIVES FOR CONVERSION

In relation to the two-level discourse of certain Christians in the West Bank and Christian education as well (see also chapter 1 in this book), one possible interpretation saw these as ways to ensure a secular if largely Muslim-led society that formed identity largely around nationalism—whether in terms of Palestinianness or Arabness (both words being used often), rather than having two separate communities (one Christian, one Muslim) that center their identities around religion, though they happen to speak the same language and have limited common customs. Conversion from Islam to Christianity, and openly inviting Muslims to consider the real option of conversion, likewise can be interpreted as political strategies, though these activities (conversion and evangelism) should never be simply reduced to political or social motives. People who engage in conversion and evangelism tend to envision Islam in its orthodox and traditional forms, as mentioned above, as irredeemable and ultimately incapable of producing a just society.

In the context of Israel-Palestine, "authentic Islam" is supposedly constructed on the pattern of the life of the Prophet, who was, in the view of most ex-Muslims, a violent, misogynistic, insecure, and intolerant individual. Any attempt to construct a just social order upon a religious politics that understands such an individual to be "the ideal man" or "*al insaan al kaamil*" is destined *ab initio* to fail. The solution is obvious then: change people's minds, and help people who have changed their minds. This is an identifiable arena in which agency is exercised in Israel-Palestine by limited numbers of Christians. Even the simple act of praying for Muslims to become Christians is an act of agency, at least from the point of view of the Christian who believes that prayer can really affect the world today. In spite of this, praying for the salvation of Muslims is exceedingly rare, including among evangelicals, though there are exceptions.[9]

While there are studies relating to the question of why Muslims convert to Christianity,[10] of particular interest here is a study done by South African missiologist Anthony Greenham entitled "A Study of Palestinian Muslim Conversions to Christ."[11] Greenham interviewed some twenty-two people in Israel-Palestine, divided evenly between men and women,

9. Miller, "Boundaries of Evangelicalism."

10. Woodberry, Shubin, and Marks, "Why Muslims Follow Jesus"; Gaudeul, *Called from Islam.*

11. Greenham, "A Study of Palestinian Muslim Conversions."

and found that the "core conversion factors" were 1. the person of Jesus Christ (22/22), 2. God's miraculous involvement in their life (16/22), 3. the truth of Jesus' message (16/22), and 4. the role of other Christian believers (13/22).[12] Political instability and rejection of Islam were each only mentioned by three persons. This means that, at least among Greenham's interviewees, conversion was primarily driven by turning to Jesus and his message and only secondarily by turning away from Islam, its Prophet and its politics. The ultimate selling point of the Christian faith appears to be, quite definitely, the person of Jesus Christ. This finding coincides with conversations and interviews I have had with CMBs both form Israel-Palestine and elsewhere. The centrality of the personality and teaching of Jesus does not, however, make this a solitary and private journey, as is seen in the fact that "the role of other believers" was mentioned by over half of Greenham's converts. Converts I know had similar experiences: the young lady from the Galilee who had an outgoing and virtuous Christian co-worker who answered her questions; the European missionary who provided a Bible in Arabic to the young seeker from the West Bank; the Arab guesthouse operator who continually prayed for and with the young student in Haifa, these are other examples.

Greenham's findings imply that we should not see conversion from Islam to Christianity as primarily a political discourse of criticism directed at Islam, but rather as a claim to have found something new, hope-giving, nourishing and peaceful in Jesus Christ that was not felt to be available in Islam. That the shari'a will not allow for this turning from the old to the new to take place in a peaceful and secure manner only later elicits efforts to undermine the shari'a as detailed in §4.

6. CONCLUSION

In sum, in relation to the freedom of CMBs, the structures of the shari'a and Islamic intolerance are the main limiting factors. Another one, and one that Christians are in a better position to actually address, though, is the fact that churches often reject the seeker or the convert. One believer from the West Bank related how a priest had threatened to call the police on him if he kept on coming to his church. The sense of anomie that Kraft[13] found in her study of Egyptian and Lebanese converts likewise applies to

12. Ibid., 172.

13. Kraft, *Searching for Heaven.*

converts in Israel-Palestine. The activity of converting compromises the relationships that previously existed, and so new relationships need to be formed to replace those and to provide a medium wherein socialization and identity-formation (as a Christian) can take place. Converts often *feel* a great sense of internal emotional and spiritual liberation/freedom in discarding Islam for Christ. The challenge to the churches in Israel-Palestine is to be a home where that new identity can flourish, and where, if possible, other challenges facing the convert, from physical danger to the loss of a job, can be addressed as well. To date, most churches, including evangelical ones, have not been up to this challenging task.

CHAPTER 7

Bibliography for Arabophone Christianity in Israel-Palestine

by Philip Sumpter

INTRODUCTION

THIS BIBLIOGRAPHY SEEKS TO provide an extensive list of publications that deal with "Arabophone Christianity" in Israel and what may be called "Palestine" (i.e., the West Bank and Gaza). Beyond the fairly clear categories "Christian" (by which I refer to those denominations which endorse the Apostle's creed) and "Israel-Palestine," two further criteria were needed in order to limit the scope of material considered relevant; these are the criteria of language and date.

I have decided to delimit the Israeli-Palestinian Christians under study in terms of their mother tongue, namely Arabic, as this appears to be the most problem-free way of lumping together the host of Christian groups found in the region while, at the same time, excluding those groups which I have decided not to consider, namely various types of "Jewish Christian" (Messianic Jews, Hebrew Catholics) and the various foreign aid workers, pilgrims and tourists that visit and remain in the country (upon whom there is plenty of research). If I had used the ethnic term "Arab," I would have had to exclude those native Christians who consciously see themselves as Syriac, Coptic, or Ethiopian, for example, often in explicit contrast to the category "Arab." If I had used the phrase "Palestinian Christianity," I would have to exclude those Arabophone inhabitants of the State of Israel who wish to define themselves as "Israelis" rather than "Palestinians" (understanding the latter term to be primarily political rather than cultural or geographical). As such, we are left with the fairly anemic yet safe category of "Arabophone," as Arabic is the universal language of all "Arab" Christians in the region, regardless of denomination or ethnicity (actual or perceived).[1] It should be pointed out, however, that this limitation is of a purely pragmatic nature, as the faith and practice of foreign aid workers and Messianic Jews, for example, do have a deep impact on Arabophone Christianity.[2] When Messianic Jewish authors and issues do appear in the bibliography, for example, it is only on the condition that the piece concerned is consciously interacting with Arabophone Christian concerns.[3]

The other additional criterion is suggested by the geo-political limitation: I have decided to only consider material post-dating the establishment of the State of Israel in 1948. Although this cut-off point does in fact represent a significant watershed in the history of the region, this decision is ultimately pragmatic in nature, for all cultural phenomena need to be analyzed in terms of their historical development; the long history of Muslim-Christian or Arab-Jewish relations leading up to 1948, for example, have clearly had an impact of the trajectories that later historical and cultural developments have taken (see chapter 1 in this book!).[4]

A further limitation concerns the kinds of material referenced. For a start, I have not included archival material, book reviews, works published solely on the Internet or articles published in parish letters, newspapers, magazines etc. An excellent bibliography of this kind of material as it relates

1. I guess that if an Arabic speaking Jewish Christian congregation should one day come into existence and receive coverage I will treat them in the bibliography.

2. It was with a heavy heart, for example, that I did not include Michael J. Pragai's, *Sie sollen wieder wohnen in ihrem Land: die Rolle von Christen bei der Heimkehr der Juden ins Land Israel* (Gerlingen: Bleicher, 1990).

3. The text book by Richard Harvey, *Mapping Messianic Jewish Theology: A Constructive Approach* (Studies in Messianic Jewish Theology; Milton Keynes: Paternoster, 2009), for example, has only a single paragraph dealing with indigenous Arabs, Christian or not, so I have not included it.

4. It was thus with a heavy heart that I was forced to excise, for example, Helen Bryer's "Arab Orthodox Christians of Jerusalem and Palestine in the Inter-War Period: A Study in Religious and Political Identity and Church-State Relations" (in Anthony O'Mahony, ed. *Christianity in the Middle East: Studies in Modern History, Theology and Politics*. London: Melisende, 2008).

to "contextual Palestinian theology" can be found in the *Literaturverzeichnis* at the end of Uwe Gräbe's *Kontextuelle palästinensische Theologie* (1999). I have also not chased up all the various translations that have been made of various books. More significantly, I have not included those journal articles that are published in journals entirely dedicated to our subject matter, nor those articles published in the conference volumes published by The Al-Liqa' Center for Religious and Heritage Studies in the Holy Land. Again, this is a pragmatic decision, as I would otherwise have to cite every article ever published in each of these series. Instead, I have a special section towards the end of the bibliography listing journals of relevance whose archives are highly worth searching. I have included the conference volumes in the section "Multi-Author Edited Volumes." Despite these seemingly objective constraints, there were still subjective and uncertain decisions that had to be made in the selection of books and articles. For example, there are books by Western Evangelicals that are concerned to advocate for Palestinian Christians by attacking Christian Zionist theologies of the land. Do these works belong in a bibliography of Arabophone Palestinian/Israeli Christianity, or are they just a matter of foreigners thinking about local issues but for the sake of their own, essentially alien concerns? I decided to include those written by authors such as Gary Burge (2003) who are particularly involved with local Arabophone life, while not including works written from a more disengaged perspective, treating the consequences of their analyses for local Arabophone theology as implications at best.[5] No doubt my readers will find much to fault here. Again, the question arose as to whether should I include works on subjects apparently unconnected to the subject of this bibliography but written *by* local Arabophone Christians. Obviously a book on plasma research by a Palestinian Christian physicist would be far off topic, but Yohanna Katanacho is a politically aware Palestinian Israeli biblical scholar whose articles on the category of "Arab" in the

5. There is a wealth of literature on the theology of the land. For example, I have not included Walter Brueggemann, *The Land: Place as Gift, Promise, and Challenge in Biblical Faith* (Overtures to Biblical Theology; 2nd ed.; Minneapolis: Augsburg, 2002), as he does not deal with Arabophone Israeli-Palestinian Christianity or theology. I did include the volume on the Land by Neuhaus/Marchadour (2007), however, for they are both inhabitants of the area (even if not indigenous) and are leaders in the local Catholic church. Or another example: I do include Wagner's *Anxious for Armageddon* (1995), as he is in more explicit dialogue with Palestinian theology than, say, W. Eugene March, *Israel and the Politics of the Land: A Theological Case Study* (foreword by Walter Brueggemann. Louisville: Westminster John Knox, 1994), as this book is written more for Westerners out of a Western perspective.

Old Testament and the function of Ps 89 in the Psalter are clearly related to his political-theological context. He is also a teacher in Bethlehem Bible College and Nazareth Evangelical College. As such, I decided to include his works.

Two further limitations on my research are the fact that I often had to judge a book or an article by its title, not having the time to read everything listed. This may have led to the inclusion or exclusion of the wrong material. A further limitation is linguistic: I have only been able to include a smattering of Hebrew and Arabic articles. This limitation pains me most, as this is in fact the language of the people who are the subject of this bibliography.

A final word about the way I have structured the material. First, I have divided the material into type of publication (see the table of contents above). Second, I have arranged the material chronologically, according to date of publication (with the most recent first), rather than alphabetically, according to author. In a land such as Israel-Palestine that is so keyed in to world events and subject to regular upheavals and change, I felt that a chronological arrangement would provide the additional service of helping the researcher discern what kinds of issues were being addressed and at what point in time. My only criterion, however, was the *year* of publication and not the month. This means that publications grouped under the same year may not be absolutely in the right chronological sequence.

BOOKS

Katanacho, Yohanna. *The Land of Christ: A Palestinian Cry*. Bethlehem: Bethlehem Bible College, 2012. Repr., Pickwick Publications, 2013.

Mansour, Atallah. *Still Waiting for the Dawn*. CreateSpace Independent Publishing Platform, 2013.

Amnon, Ramon. נצרות ונוצרים במדינת היהודים: המדיניות הישראלית הכנסיות והקהילות הנוצריות 2010–1948)). (*Christians and Christianity in the Jewish State: Israeli Policy towards the Churches and the Christian Communities [1948–2010]*). The JIIS Studies series 420. Jerusalem: The Jerusalem Institute for Israel Studies, 2012.

Fisher, Julia. *Meet Me at the Olive Tree: Stories of Jews and Arabs Reconciled to the Messiah*. Oxford: Monarch, 2012.

Kuruvilla, Samuel J. *Radical Christianity in Palestine and Israel: Liberation and Theology in the Middle East*. Library of Modern Religion 19. London: Tauris Academic Studies, 2012.

Younan, Munib A. *Our Shared Witness: A Voice for Justice and Reconciliation*. Edited by Fred Strickert. Minneapolis: Lutheran University Press, 2012.

Berge, Gied ten. *Land van mensen: christenen, joden en moslims tussen confrontaties en dialoog*. Nijmegen: Valkhof Pers, 2011.

Farah, Fuad D. *Christian presence in the Holy Land*. Nazareth: Fuad Farah, 2011.

Kassis, Rifat Odeh. *Kairos for Palestine*. Panjim, Goa: Badayl-Alternatives, 2011.

Kincaid, Jack, and Ron Brackin. *Between Two Fires: The Untold Story of Palestinian Christians*. 2d ed.; ePublishers: Weller & Bunsby, 2011.

Mansour, Botrus. *When Your Neighbour is the Saviour*. Pasadena: Hope Publishing House, 2011.

McGahern, Una. *Palestinian Christians in Israel: State Attitudes towards Non-Muslims in a Jewish State*. Durham Modern Middle East and Islamic World Series 22. London: Routledge, 2011.

McRay, Jonathan. *You Have Heard It Said: Events of Reconciliation*. Eugene, OR: Resource Publications, 2011.

Rowden, Rebecca. *Baptists in Israel: The Letters of Paul and Marjorie Rowden 1952–1957*. Nahville: Fields Publishing.

Schweizerischer Evangelischer Kirchenbund. *The Churches of the Middle East: Working toward Peace*. Bern: Publisher Federation of Swiss Protestant Churches FSPC, 2011.

Aghazarian, Elise, Andrea Merli, Lucia Russo & Ingeborg Tiemann. *Rachel's Tomb: An Alien in Her Hometown? Perceptions from the Other Side of the Wall*. Monographs of Middle Eastern History and Presence. Berlin: AphorismA Verlag, 2010.

Giddings, Philip James. *Reflecting on Kairos Palestine: A Word of Faith, Hope and Love from the Heart of Palestinian Suffering*. General Synod papers, Series 11. "Mission and Public Affairs Council." London : General Synod of the Church of England, 2010.

Karios Palestine; Israel/Palestine Mission Network of the Presbyterian Church (U.S.A.). *Kairos Palestine: A Moment of Truth*. Pittsburgh, PA: Israel/Palestine Mission Network of the Presbyterian Church (U.S.A.), 2010.

Kildani, Hanna. *Modern Christianity in the Holy Land*. Bloomington: AuthorHouse, 2010.

May, Melanie A. *Jerusalem Testament: Palestinian Christians Speak, 1988–2008*. Grand Rapids: Eerdmans, 2010.

Nijim, Fuad Bassim. *Hope is my Gift to You*. Bethlehem: Diyar, 2010.

Yousef, Mossab Hassan. *Son of Hamas: A Gripping Account of Terror, Betrayal, Political Intrigue, and Unthinkable Choices*. Carol Stream, IL: SaltRiver, 2010.

Ricks, Thomas M. *Eyewitness to Turbulent Times in Palestine: The Ramallah Diaries of Khalil Totah, 1886–1955*. Ramallah: Institute of Jerusalem Studies, 2009.

Sabbah, Michel. *Faithful Witness: On Reconciliation and Peace in the Holy Land*. Hyde Park: New City Press, 2009.

Ateek, Naim Stifan. *A Palestinian Christian Cry for Reconciliation*. Maryknoll, NY: Orbis Books, 2008.

Awad, Alex. *Palestinian Memories: The Story of a Palestinian Mother and Her People*. Bethlehem: Bethlehem Bible College, 2008.

Chacour, Elias, with Alain Michel. *Faith Beyond Despair: Building Hope in the Holy Land*. Translated and edited by Anthony Harvey. Norwich: Canterbury Press, 2008.

Chorherr, Christa. *Wessen Heiliges Land? Christen im Israel-Palästina-Konflikt*. Wien : Braumüller, 2008.

Cohen, R. *Saving the Holy Sepulchre: How Rival Christians Came Together to Rescue Their Holiest Shrine*. Oxford: Oxford University Press, 2008.

Dass, Ramsay. *Middle East Christians: The Untold Story*. Oak Park, MI: American Middle East Christian Congress, 2008.

Gianazza, Pier Giorgio. *Guida alle comunità cristiane in Terra Santa: Diversità e fede nei luoghi di Gesù*. Bologna: EDB, 2008.

Hammond, Constance A. *Shalom/Salaam/Peace: A Liberation Theology of Hope*. Religion and Violence. Sheffield: Equinox, 2008.

Katanacho, Yohanna. أنا هو . . . فمن أنت؟ عبارة "أنا هو" في انجيل يوحنا. (*I Am . . . So Who Are You? The "I am" Sayings in the Gospel of John*). 2d ed.; Jerusalem: Christian and Missionary Alliance, 2008.

Zaru, Jean. *Occupied with Nonviolence: A Palestinian Woman Speaks*. Forward by Rosemary Radford Ruether. Minneapolis: Fortress, 2008.

Dupeyron, Catherine. *Chrétiens en terre sainte: disparition ou mutation?* Paris: Albin Michel, 2007.

Farhat-Naser, Sumaya. *Disteln im Weinberg: Tagebuch aus Palästina*. Zurich: Lenos, 2007.

Har-El, Menashe. *Three religions and their contribution to Jerusalem and the land of Israel*. Policy papers (Merkaz Ari'el le-meḥḳere mediniyut) 169. Shaarei Tikva: Ariel Center for Policy Research, 2007.

Jamal, A. *Arab Minority Nationalism in Israel: The Politics of Indigeneity*. London: Routledge, 2011.

Karabell, Zachary. *Peace Be Upon You: The Story of Muslim, Christian, and Jewish Coexistence*. New York: Alfred A. Knopf, 2007.

Marchadour, Alain and David Neuhaus. *The Land, the Bible, and History: "Toward the Land that I Will Show You ."* The Abrahamic Dialogues Series. New York: Fordham University Press, 2007.

Raheb, Mitri. *God's Reign and People's Rule*. Berlin: Aphorisma, 2007.

Strickert, Fred. *Rachel Weeping: Jews, Christians and Muslims at the Fortress Tomb*. Collegeville, MN: Liturgical Press, 2007.

Duphil, Alain. *Au pays de Jésus: les chrétiens—et la lignée d'Abraham : essai*. Nantes : Editions Amalthée, 2006.

Kassis, Rifat Odeh. *Palestine: A Bleeding Wound in the World's Conscience*. Ramallah: Bailasan, 2006.

Khoury, Geries Sa'ed. عرب مسيحيون: أصالة—حضور—انفتاح (*Arab Christians: Rootedness—Presence—Openness*). Jerusalem: Al-Liqa Centre for Religious Studies in the Holy Land, 2006.

Lutz, Charles P. and Robert Ora Smith. *Christians and a Land Called Holy: How We Can Foster Justice, Peace, and Hope*. Minneapolis: Fortress, 2006.

Munayer, Salim. *Reconciliation and the Cross*. Jerusalem: Musalaha, 2006.

Nerel, Gershon. *Anti-Zionism in the "Electronic Church" of Palestinian Christianity*. Analysis of Current Trends in Antisemitism 27. Jerusalem: SICSA, 2006.

Reitsma, Bernhard J.G. *Wie is onze God? Arabische christenen, Israël en de aard van God*. Boekencentrum Essay. Zoetermeer: Boekencentrum, 2006.

Bialer, U. *Cross on the Star of David: The Christian World in Israel's Foreign Policy, 1948–1967*. Jerusalem: Yad Yitzhak Ben Zvi, 2007 (in Hebrew).

Destani, B. *Minorities in the Middle East: Religious communities in Jerusalem, 1843–1974 and minorities in Israel*. Minorities in the Middle East, an archival survey. Slough: Archive Editions, 2005.

Farhat- Naser, Sumaya. *Verwurzelt im Land der Olivenbäume: Eine Palästinenserin im Streit für den Frieden*. Lenos Pocket. Lenos: Zurich, 2005.

Raheb, Mitri. *Bethlehem hinter Mauern*. Guetersloh: Guetersloher Verlaghaus, 2005.

Sabeel Liberation Theology Center (Jerusalem). *Contemporary Way of the Cross: A Liturgical Journey along the Palestinian Via Dolorosa*. Jerusalem: Sabeel Palestinian Liberation Theology Center, 2005.

Weiner, Justus Reid. *Human Rights Of Christians In Palestinian Society.*Jerusalem: Jerusalem Center for Public Affairs, 2005.

Hojaiban, Jenifer. *Palestinian Christians in Struggle.* Jerusalem: YMCA of Palestine. East Jerusalem YMCA, 2004.

Mansour, Atallah. *Narrow Gate Churches: The Christian Presence in the Holy Land under Muslim and Jewish Rule.* Pasadena: Hope Publishing House, 2004.

Rahal, Carolyn. *The Palestinian Christians: A Population in Decline.* Washington, D.C.: Georgetown University, 2004

Raheb, Mitri. *Bethalehem Besieged: Stories of Hope in Times of Trouble.* Minneapolis: Fortress, 2004

Raheb, Mitri. *Christ und Palästinenser.* Berlin: Aphorisma, 2004.

Shorrosh, Anis. *Islam: A threat or a Challenge?* Fairhope, AL: Nall, 2004.

Burge, Gary M. *Whose Land? Whose Promise? What Christians Are Not Being Told about Israel and the Palestinians.* Cleveland: Pilgrim, 2003.

Chacour, Elias. *Blood Brothers: The Dramatic Story of a Palestinian Christian Working for Peace in Israel.* 2d and enl. ed. Grand Rapids, MI: Chosen Books, 2003.

Hammer, Joshua. *A Season in Bethlehem: Unholy War in a Sacred Place.* London: Free Press, 2003

Maalouf, Tony. *Arabs in the Shadow of Israel: The Unfolding of God's Prophetic Plan for Ishmael's Line.* Grand Rapids, MI: Kregel Publications, 2003..

Odeh, Yousif. ألمجيء الثاني للمسيح: تفسير النصوص البوية عاى ضوء كلمة الله. *(The Second Coming of Christ: Interpretation of Prophetic Texts According to the Word of God).* Kfar Yassif: Yousif Odeh, 2003.

Pedersen, Kirsten Stoffregen. *The Holy Land Christians.* Jerusalem : K. Stoffregen-Pedersen, 2003

Rolin, Jean. *Christians in Palestine.* Translated by Marjolijn de Jager. Brooklyn, NY: Ig Pub., 2006. Translation of Rolin, *Chrétiens.* Paris: P.O.L., 2003.

Sennott, Charles M. *The Body and the Blood: The Middle East's Vanishing Christians and the Possibility for Peace.* New York: PublicAffairs, 2003.

Younan, Munib. *Witnessing for Peace: In Jerusalem and the World.* Edited by Fred Strickert. Minneapolis: Fortress, 2003.

Biestmann-Kotte, Dirk. *Die Menschen, das Land und der Ölzweig: Palästinensische Christen für Frieden und Gerechtigkeit.* Kleine Schriftenreihe des Kulturvereins AphorismA, special issue 10. With a preface by Viola Raheb; Trier: Kulturverein AphorismA, 2002.

Dumper, Michael. *The Politics of Sacred Space: The Old City of Jerusalem in the Middle East Conflict.* London: Lynne Rienner, 2002.

Farah, Rafiq A. *Troubled Waters: A History of the Anglican Church in Jerusalem, 1841–1998.* Leicester: Christian Aware, 2002.

Gopin, Marc. *Holy War, Holy Peace: How Religion Can Bring Peace to the Middle East.* Oxford: Oxford University Press, 2002.

Habiby, Emile. *The Secret Life of Saeed: The Pessoptimist.* Trans. by S. Khadra-Jayyusi. New York: Interlink Books, 2002.

Halevi, Yossi Klein. *At the Entrance to the Garden of Eden: A Jew's Search for God with Christians and Muslims in the Holy Land.* New York: Harper Collins, 2002.

Israeli, Raphael. *Green Crescent over Nazareth: The Displacement of Christians by Muslims in the Holy Land.* Cass series—Israeli History, Politics, and Society. London: Frank Cass, 2002.

Janin, Hunt. *Four Paths to Jerusalem: Jewish, Christian, Muslim, and Secular Pilgrimages, 1000 BCE to 2001 CE.* Jefferson, NC: McFarland & Co., 2002.

Katanacho, Yohanna and Dina Katanacho. أطلقوني: دور ومكانة المرأة في المسيحية *(Free Me: The Role and Status of Women in Christianity).* Jerusalem: Christian and Missionary Alliance, 2002.

Philpott, Ellie. *Sur le chemin étroit : Israël et Palestine, quelques témoignages de foi chrétienne au coeur du conflit.* Strasbourg : Portes ouvertes; Valence Ligue pour la lecture de la Bible, 2002

Schiller, Ely. *Christianity and Christians in Eretz-Israel.* Ariel. Jerusalem: Ariel, 2002.

Shorrosh, Anis. *The True Furqan.* 3d ed. Duncanville, TX: World Wide Printing, 2002.

Ghanem, A. *The Palestinian-Arab Minority in Israel, 1948—2000: A Political Study.* New York: SUNY Press, 2001.

Sennott, Charles M. *The Body and the Blood: The Holy Land's Christians at the Turn of a New Millennium : A Reporter's Journey.* New York: PublicAffairs, 2001.

Merkley, Paul Charles. *Christian Attitudes towards the State of Israel.* McGill-Queen's Studies in the History of Religion: Series Two. Montreal: McGill-Queens University Press, 2001.

Wager, Donald E. *Dying in the Land of Promise: Palestine and Palestinian Christianity from Pentecost to 2000.* London: Melisende, 2001.

Awad, Alex. *Through the Eyes of the Victims: The Story of the Arab-Israeli Conflict.* Forward by Naim Ateek. Bethlehem: Bethlehem Bible College, 2001.

Bechmann, Ulrike. *Vom Dialog zur Solidarität—Das christlich-islamische Gespräch in Palästina.* Kleine Schriftenreihe des Kulturvereins AphorismA, special issue 6. Trier: Kulturverein AphorismA, 2000.

Benvenisti, Meron. *Sacred Landscape: the Buried History of the Holy Land since 1948.* Trans. by
Maxine Kaufman-Lacusta. Berkeley: University of California Press, 2000.

Berkowitz, Shmuel. *The Battle for the Holy Places: The Struggle over Jerusalem and the Holy Sites in Israel, Judea, Samaria and the Gaza District.* Jerusalem: Hed Arzi, 2000.

Friesen, LeRoy. *Mennonite Witness in the Middle East: A Missiological Introduction.* Elkhart, IN: Mennonite Board of Missions, 2000.

Heyer, Friedrich. *2000 Jahre Kirchengeschichte des Heiligen Landes: Märtyrer, Mönche, Kirchenväter, Kreuzfahrer, Patriarchen, Ausgräber und Pilger.* Studien zur Orientalischen Kirchengeschichte 11. 2d ed.; Stuttgart: LIT Verlag, 2000.

Munayer, Salim J. *The Ethnic Identity of Palestinian Arab Christian Adolescents in Israel.* Oxford: Oxford Center for Mission Studies and University of Wales, 2000.

Prolongeau, Hubert. *Le curé de Nazareth: Emile Shoufani, Arabe israélien, homme de parole en Galilée* Paris, Albin Michel : 2000.

Said, Edward W. *Out of Place: A Memoir.* New York: Vintage Books, 2000.

Zeyadeh, Nicola. المسيحيّة والعرب *(Christianity and the Arabs).* Damascus, 2000.

Arafat, Jamil. من قرانا المهجرة في الجليل *(From our Deserted Arab Villages in Galillee).* Nazareth, 1999.

El-Assal , Riah Abu. *Caught in Between: The Story of an Arab Palestinian Christian Israeli.* London: SPCK, 1999.

Gräbe, Uwe. *Kontextuelle palästinensische Theologie: Streitbare und umstrittene Beiträge zum ökumenischen und interreligiösen Gespräch.* Missionswissenschaftliche Forschungen. New Series 9. Erlangen: Erlanger Verlag für Mission und Ökumene, 1999.

Hilliard, Alison, and Betty Jane Bailey. *Living Stones Pilgrimage with the Christians of the Holy Land*. London: University of Notre Dame Press, 1999.

Al Bann, George Istefan Youssef المغتربون والمهجرون: المسيحيون الى أين؟ *(The Christians Who Live Abroad and Those Who Immigrated: Where to?)*. Amman, 1998.

Degany, Rami. כנסיות, עדות ומסדרים נוצריים בישראל (*Churches, Denominations, and Christian Orders in Israel*). Ariel,1999.

Feldtkeller, Andreas. *Die "Mutter der Kirchen" im "Haus des Islam": gegenseitige Wahrnehmung von arabischen Christen und Muslimen im West- und Ostjordanland*. Missionswissenschaftliche Forschungen. New Series 6. Erlangen: Erlanger Verlag für Mission und Ökumene, 1998.

Khoury, Rafiq. تجسد كنائس الشرق في الخيمة العربية : مقارنات من الزاوية الفلسطينية. *(The Incarnation of the Eastern Church in the Arab Tent: A Comparison from a Palestinian Perspective)*. Jerusalem: Al-Liqa Centre for Religious Studies in the Holy Land, 1998.

LAW (Organization: Jerusalem). *The Myth of Christian Persecution by the Palestinian Authority*. Jerusalem: Palestinian Society for the Protection of Human Rights and the Environment, 1998.

Neubert-Preine, T. *100 Jahre Evangelisch-Lutherische Erlöserkirche in Jerusalem*. Jerusalem: Evang.-luth. Propstei, 1998.

Nieswandt, Reiner. *Abrahams umkämpftes Erbe: Eine kontextuelle Studie zum modernen Konflikt von Juden, Christen und Muslimen um Israel/Palästina*. Stuttgarter Biblische Beiträge 41. Stuttgart: Verlag Katholisches Bibelwerk, 1998.

Sabella, Bernaard. *On the Eve of the New Millennium: Christian Voices from the Holy Land*. London: Palestinian General Delegation in the United Kingdom: Office of Representation of the PLO to the Holy See, 1998.

Raheb, Mitri, and Fred Strickert. *Bethlehem 2000: Past and Present*. Heidelberg: Palmyra Verlag, 1998.

Raheb, Mitri, and Fred Strickert. *Bethlehem 2000: Mehr als Stern und Stall*. Heidelberg: Palmyra Verlag,1998.

Zarley, Kermit. *Palestine is Coming: The Revival of Ancient Philistia*. Hannibal, MO: Hannibal Books, 1998.

Cragg, Kenneth. *Palestine: The Prize and Price of Zion*. London: Cassell, 1997.

Ellis, Marc H. *Über den jüdisch-christlichen Dialog hinaus: Solidarität mit dem palästinensischen Volk*. Kleine Schriftenreihe des Kulturvereins AphorismA 4; 3d ed.; Trier: Kulturverein AphorismA, 1997.

Ellis, Marc H. *Über den jüdisch-christlichen Dialog hinaus: Aus der Werkstatt eines jüdischen Befreiungstheologen*. Kleine Schriftenreihe des Kulturvereins AphorismA 4; Trier: Kulturverein AphorismA, 1997.

Karen, A. *Jerusalem: One City, Three Faiths*. New York: Random House, 1997.

Ramon, Amnon. הגורים הנוצרי ושאלת ירושלים *(Christian Views on the Jerusalem Question)*. דפי רקע לקובעי מדיניות (Background Papers for Policy Makers). Jerusalem: The Jerusalem Institute for Israel Studies, 1997.

Ramon, Amnon and Rotem Giladi. מודל הותיקן ושאלת ירושלים *(The Model of the Vatican and the Question of Jerusalem)*. דפי רקע לקובעי מדיניות (Background Papers for Policy Makers). Jerusalem: The Jerusalem Institute for Israel Studies, 1997.

Rabinowitz, Dan. *Overlooking Nazareth: The Ethnography of Exclusion in Galilee*. Cambridge Studies in Social and Cultural Anthropology. Cambridge: Cambridge University Press, 1997.

Sassar, Jaber Mussa, Al-Mujeidel. *Wo ist mein Dorf? Die Geschichte eines palästinensichen Lutheraners und seines verschwundenen Dorfes*. Published by Hans-Joachim Uhle in the autumn of 1997 as an unedited manuscript in connection with the Jerusalemverein im Berliner Missionswerk. Berlin, 1997.

Farah, Najwā Qa'wār. *A Continent Called Palestine: One Woman's Story*. London: Triange, 1996.

Khoury, Geries, Adnan Musailam, and Musa Darwish. القدس: دراسات فلسطينية اسلامية ومسيحية *(Jerusalem: Muslim and Christian Palestinian Studies)*. Jerusalem, 1996.

Al-Liqa' Center for Religious Studies in the Holy Land, ed. *Jeruslaem between Religious Freedom and Political Sovereignty: A Day of Reflection*. Jerusalem: Al-Liqa`Center for religious and heritage studies in the Holy Land publications, 1995.

Ashrawi, Hanan. *This Side of Peace: A Personal Account*. New York: Simon & Schuster, 1995.

Billioud, Jean-Michel. *Histoire des Chrétien d'Orient*. Collection "Comprendre le Moyen-Orient." Paris, 1995.

Emmett, Chad F. *Beyond the Basilica: Christians and Muslims in Nazareth*. University of Chicago Geography Research Paper 237. Chicago: University of Chicago Press, 1995

Farah, Rafiq.تاريخ الكنيسة الاسقفية في مطرانية القدس *(History of the Episcopal Church in the Jerusalem Bishopric)*. Jerusalem, 1995

Farhat-Naser, Sumaya. *Thymian und Steine: Eine palästinensiche Lebensgeschichte*. Zurich: Lenos, 1995.

Raheb, Mitri. *I am a Palestinian Christian*. Minneapolis: Augsburg Fortress, 1995.

.

Soudah, Romell. *Christians in the Holy Land: Palestinian Christians in the Rural Areas, a Survey, 1994*. Bethlehem: Bethlehem University, 1995.

Talal, Hassan Ibn. *Christianity in the Arab World*. London: Arabesque, 1995. Translation of المسيحي في العالم العربي *(Christianity in the Arab World)*. Amman: Arabesque Int., 1994.

Wagner, Donald E. *Anxious for Armageddon: A Call to Partnership for Middle Eastern and Western Christians*. Forward by Elias Chacour. Scottdalte, PA: Herald Press, 1995.

Wessels, Antoine. *Arab and Christian? Christians in the Middle East*. Kampen: Kok Pharos, 1995.

Are, Thomas L. *Israeli Peace, Palestinian Justice: Liberation Theology and the Peace Process*. Atlanta: Clarity Press, 1994.

Ellis, Marc H. *Ending Auschwitz: the Future of Jewish and Christian Life*. Louisville, KY: Westminster John Knox, 1994.

Lindén, Gunilla. *Church Leadership in a Political Crisis: Joint Statements from the Jerusalem Heads of Churches 1988–1992*. Swedish Institute of Missionary Research, Mission, No. 9. Uppsala, 1994.

Pedersen, Kirsten Stoffregen, *The Ethiopian Church and its Community in Jerusalem*. Kleine Schriftenreihe des Kulturvereins AphorismA. Trier: Kulturverein AphorismA, 1994.

Raheb, Mitri. *Ich bin Christ und Palästinenser: Israel, seine Nachbarn und die Bibel*. Gütersloher Taschenbücher, 1307. Gütersloh: Gütersloher Verlagshaus, 1994.

Talal, Hasan, Ibn. المسيحي في العالم العربي *(Christianity in the Arab World)*. Amman: Arabesque Int., 1994.

Valognes, Jean-Pierre. *Vie et mort des chrétiens d'Orient: Des origins à nos jours*. Paris: Fayard, 1994.

Aburish, Saïd K. *The Forgotten Faithful: The Christians of the Holy Land*. London: Quartet Books, 1993.

Burge, Gary M. *Who are God's People in the Middle East?* Grand Rapids, MI.: Zondervan, 1993.

Damm, Thomas. *Palestinian Liberation Theology: A German Theologian's Approach and Appreciation*. Kleine Schriftenreihe des Kulturvereins AphorismA 5 E. Translated by Charlotte Methuen, with preface by Rev. Dr. Mitri Raheb. Trier: Kulturverein AphorismA, 1994.Translation of "*Palästinensische Befreiungstheologie*"*: Annäherung und Würdigung aus der Sicht eines detuschen Theologen*. Kleine Schriftenreihe des Kulturvereins AphorismA 5. Trier: Kulturverein AphorismA, 1993.

Kaldani, Hanna Said.المسيحية العربية في الاردن وفلسطين *(Arab Christianity in Jordan and Palestine*). Amman: (no publisher mentioned), 1993.

Khoury, Rafiq. *Palästinensisches Christentum: Erfahrungen und Perspektiven*. Preface by Michel Sabbah. Kleine Schriftenreihe des Kulturvereins AphorismA. Trier: Kulturverein AphorismA, 1993.

Munayer, Salim. *In the Footsteps of Our Father Abraham*. Jerusalem: Musalaha, 1993.

Osteski-Lazar, Sarah. איקרית ובירעם: הספור המלא *(Iqrit and Bira'am: The Full Story)*. Giva'at Haviva, 1993.

Sabbah, Michael. *Reading the Bible Today in the Land of the Bible*. Jerusalem: Latin Patriarchate, 1993.

Sarraf Faraj Bishara, المسيحية وغزة *(Christianity and Gaza)*. Gaza, 1993.

Rose, John H. Melkon. *Armenians of Jerusalem: Memories of Life in Palestine*. London: Radcliffe Press, 1993.

Tsimhoni, Daphne. *Christian Communities in Jerusalem and the West Bank since 1948: An Historical, Social and Political Study*. Westport, Conn.: Praeger, 1993.

Younan, Munib A. إقرار اوغسبرغ. كتاب الاقرار الرئيسي لعقائد الكنيسة الانجيلية اللوثرية. اعد التقجمة والدراسة القس منيب ا. يونان *(The Augsburg Confession in Arabic. Translated with an Elaborative Introduction by the Rev. Munib A. Younan)*. Jerusalem: Emerezian Est., 1993.

Benziman, Uzi, and Atallah Mansour. דיירי משנה (*Sub Tenants)*. Jerusalem, 1992.

Kimball, Charles A. *Angle of vision: Christians and the Middle East*. New York: Friendship Press, 1992.

Qleibo, Ali H. *Before the Mountains Disappear: An Ethnographic Chronicle of the Modern Palestinians*. Cairo: A Kloreus Book, Al-Ahram Press, 1992.

Gorkin, Michael. *Days of Honey Days of Onion: The Story of a Palestinian Family in Israel*. Boston: Beacon Press, 1991.

Romann, Michael and Alex Weingrod. *Living Together Separately: Arabs and Jews in Contemporary Jerusalem*. Princeton studies on the Near East. Princeton: Princeton University Press, 1991.

Tleel, John N. *Ecumenical Life in Jerusalem: A study sponsored by the World Council of Churches' Sub-Unit on Renewal and Congregational Life*. Geneva: World Council of Churches, 1991.

Chacour, Elias and Mary E. Jenson. *We Belong to the Land: The Story of a Palestinian Israeli Who Lives for Peace and Reconciliation*. Notre Dame: University of Notre Dame, 1990.

Christians Aware (Organization). *Palestinian Pain and Promise*. Leicester: Christians Aware, 1990.

Khoury, Geries Sa'ed. انتفاضة السما وانتفاضة الارض *(The Intifada of Heaven and the Intifada of Earth).* 2d ed.; Nazareth, 1990.

Kreutz, Andrej *Vatican Policy on the Palestinian/Israeli Conflict: The Struggle for the Holy Land.* Contributions in Political Science 246. New York: Greenwood Press, 1990.

Minns, Amina and Nadia Hijab. *Citizens Apart: A Portrait of the Palestinians in Israel.* Society and Culture in the modern Middle East. London: I.B. Tauris, 1990.

Raheb, Mitri. *Das reformatorische Erbe unter den Palästinensern: Zur Entstehung der evangelisch-lutherischen Kirche in Jordanien.* Die Lutherische Kirche. Geschichte und Gestalten 11. Gütersloh: Gütersloher Verlagshaus G. Mohn, 1990.

Rantisi, Audeh G, with Ralph K. Beebe. *Blessed Are the Peacemakers: The Story of a Palestinian Christian in the Occupied West Bank.* Grand Rapids, MI.: Zondervan, 1990.

Sabella, Bernard. *The Diocese of the Latin Patriarchate. Introductory Study of the Social, Political, Economical and Religious Situation (West Bank and Gaza Strip, Jordan, Israel and Cyprus).* Jerusalem: Latin Patriarchate Printing Press, 1990.

Ateek, Naim Stifan. *Justice and Only Justice: A Palestinian Theology of Liberation.* Maryknoll , NY: Orbis Books, 1989.

Goble, Phillip E., and Salim Munayer. *New Creation Book for Muslims.* Pasadena, CA: Mandate, 1989.

Rock, Alberto. *The Status Quo in the Holy Places.* Holy Land publications. Jerusalem: Franciscan Printing Press, 1989.

Aburish, Saïd Khalil. *Children of Bethany: The Story of a Palestinian Family.* Bloomington: Indiana University Press, 1988.

Colbi, Saul P. *A History of the Christian Presence in the Holy Land.* New York: University Press of America, 1988.

Shorrosh, Anis. *Islam Revealed: A Christian Arab's View of Islam.* Nashville: T. Nelson, 1988.

Al-Liqa Centre for Religious Studies in the Holy Land, *Theology and the Local Church in the Holy Land.* Nazareth: Al-Hakem Printing Press, 1987.

Birkland, Carol J. *Unified in Hope: Arabs and Jews Talk About Peace. Interviews by Carol J. Birkland.* Geneva: WCC Publications, 1987.

Rokach, Livia. *The Catholic Church and the Question of Palestine.* London: Saqi Books, 1987.

Schmelz. U.O. *Modern Jerusalem's Demographic Evolution.* Jerusalem: Jerusalem Institute for Israel Studies, 1987.

Irani, G.E. *The Papacy and the Middle East: The Role of the Holy See in the Arab-Israeli Conflict, 1962–1984.* Notre Dame, Indiana: 1986.

Schneider, Ursula. *Land ist unser Leben: Galiläische Dörfer im Nahostkonflikt. Soziologie und Anthropologie.* Frankfurt: Peter Lang, 1986.

Ekin, Larry. *Enduring Witness: The Churches and the Palestinians.* Geneva: W.C.C., 1985.

Laham, Lutfi. *Hoffnung auf eine Ökumene in Jerusalem.* Köln: Luthe-Verlag, 1985

Wehbe, L. *L'Église maronite.* Jerusalem: Franciscan Printing Press, 1985.

Azarya, V. *The Armenian Quarter of Jerusalem: Urban Life Behind Monastery Walls.* Berkely, 1984.

Pedersen, Kirsten Stoffregen. *The History of the Ethiopian Community in the Holy Land from the Time of Emperor Tewodros II till 1974.* Studia oecumenica Hierosolymitana 2. Jerusalem: Tantur Ecumenical Institute, 1983.

Médebielle, Pierre. *Gaza et son histoire chrétienne.* Jérusalem : Impremerie du pariarcat latin, 1982.

King, Michael Christopher. *The Palestinians and the Churches,* 3 vols. (1948–56; 1956–67; 1967–74; *1948–1956*). Commission on Inter-Church Aid, Refugee and World Service. Geneva: World Council of Churches, 1981–1985.

Prittie, Terence. *Whose Jerusalem.* London: Frederick Muller Ltd, 1981.

Samir, S. Khalil. *La tradition arabe chrétienne et la chrétienté de Terre-Sainte.* Jerusalem: Institut oecuménique de recherches théologiques, 1980.

Shorrosh, Anis. *Jesus, Prophecy & Middle East.* Daphne, AL: Anis Shorrosh Evangelistic Association, 1979.

Jean Corbon, *L'Église des Arabes.* Paris: Éditions du Cerf, 1977.

Rock, Alberto. *Lo Statu Quo dei Luoghi Santi.* Jerusalem: Franciscan Printing Press, 1977.

Benvenisti, M. *Jerusalem: The Torn City.* Minneapolis: Israeltypset and the University of Minneapolis, 1976.

Hintlian, Kevork. *History of the Armenians in the Holy Land.* Jerusalem: St. James Press, 1976.

Issa, A.O. *Les minorités chrétiennes de Palestine.* Jerusalem: Franciscan Printing Press, 1976.

Koriah, Yacoub, *The Syrian Orthodox Church in the Holy Land.* Jerusalem: St. Mark's Monastery, 1976.

Karkenny, J.K. *The Syrian Orthodox Church in the Holy Land.* Jerusalem, 1976.

Odeh, Issa Anton. *Les minorités chrétiennes de Palestine à travers les siècles, étude historico-juridique et développement moderne international.* Jerusalem: Franciscan Printing Press, 1976.

Barth, Markus. *Der Jude Jesus, Israel und die Palästinenser.* Zürich: TVZ, 1975.

Hefley, James C., and Marti Hefley. *The Liberated Palestinian: The Anis Shorrosh Story.* Wheaton, Ill.: Victor, 1975.

Mansour, Atallah. *Still Waiting for the Dawn: An Autobiography.* London: Martin Secker & Warburg Ltd, 1975.

Pedersen, K. *Ethiopian Institutions in Jerusalem.* Jerusalem, 1975.

Pope Paul VI. *Apostolic exhortation of His Holiness Paul VI to the Bishops, clergy and faithful of the world concerning the increased needs of the Church in the Holy land, Nobis in Animo, March 25, 1974.* Washington : Publications Office, United States Catholic Conferences, 1974.

Cohen, Erik and Hermona Grunau. *Survey of Minorities in Israel.* Jerusalem: Hebrew University of Jerusalem, 1972.

Colbi, Saul P. *Cristianesimo in Terra Santa: Passato e presente.* Translated by Elsa Codronchi Torelli. Roma: Coines, 1972.

Colbi, Saul P. *The Growth and Development of Christian Church Institutions in the State of Israel.* Jerusalem: Israel Economist, 1972.

Löhr, Detlef. *Christen heute im Heiligen Land: ein Reiseführer.* Erlanger Taschenbücher 16. Erlangen : Verlag der Ev.-Luth. Mission, 1971.

Zander, Walter. *Israel and the Holy Places of Christendom.* London: Weidenfeld & Nicolson, 1971.

Østerbye, Per. *The Church in Israel: A Report on the Work and Position of the Christian Churches in Israel, with Special Reference to the Protestant Churches and Communities.* Studia missionalia Upsaliensia 15. Lund: Gleerup, 1970.

Runciman, Steven. *The Historic Role of the Christian Arabs of Palestine.* Carreras Arab lecture, 1968. London: Longman Group, 1970.

Carter, John T. *Witness in Israel, the story of Paul Rawden.* Nashville, Tennessee: Broadman Press, 1969.

Colbi, Saul P. *Christian Churches in Israel.* Jerusalem: Israel Economist, 1969.

Colbi, Saul P. *Christianity in the Holy Land: Past and Present.* Tel Aviv: Am Hassefer, 1969.

Runciman, Steven. *The Chrisitan Arabs in Palestine.* London: Longman, 1969.

Al A'yeb, Salwa Balhaj Saleh. المسيحية العربية وتطورها *(Arab Christianity and its Evolution).* Beirut, 1968.

Antreassian, Assadour. *Jerusalem and the Armenians.* Jerusalem: St. James Press, 1968.

Heinrici, Fritz. *Wir haben einen Gott, der da hilft: Missionserlebnisse im Heiligen Land.* Schorndorf: Verlag der Evangelischen Karmelmission, 1966.

Colbi, Saul P. *A Short History of Christianity in the Holy Land.* Jerusalem: Am Hassefer, 1965.

Medebielle, P. *The Diocese of the Latin Patriarchate of Jerusalem.* Jerusalem, 1963.

Medebielle, P. *Encore a Propos du Patriarchat Latin de Jerusalem.* Jerusalem, 1962.

Baker, Dwight L. *Baptist Golden Jubilee: 50 Years in Palestine-Israel.* Baptist Village, Israel: Baptist Convention in Israel, 1961.

Patriarchate Grec Melkite CAtholique d'Antioche et de tout l'Orient et d'Alexandrie et de Jérusalem. *Catholicisme ou Latinisme?* Harissa, 1961.

Taslitt, Israel Isaac. *Faith Walks the Land: The Christian Community in Israel.* Cleveland: Reniarc Associates, 1961.

Meinardus, Otto. *The Copts in Jerusalem.* Cairo: Commission on Oecumenical Affairs of the See of Alexandria, 1960.

Al-Hudhayfi, H. *Ta'rikh al-Qadiyya al-'Arabiyya al-Urthudhuksiyya.* Amman, 1957.

Hajjar, J. *L'Apostolat des Missionaires Latins dans le Proche-Orient selon les Directives Romaines.* Jerusalem, 1956.

Moschopoulos, N. *La Terre Sainte: Essai sur l'histoire politique et diplomatique des Lieux Saints de la chrétienté.* Athens: N. Moschopoulos, 1956.

Foley, Rolla, *Song of the Arab: The Religious Ceremonies, Shrines, and Folk Music of the Holy Land Christian Arab.* London: Macmillan, 1953.

Wardi, Chaim. *Christians in Israel: A Survey.* Jerusalem: Ministry of Religious Affairs, 1950.

Appeal by the Committee of the Christian Union of Palestine: Addressed to All World Religious and Political Bodies. New York: Arab Higher Committee Delegation for Palestine, 1948

MULTI-AUTHOR EDITED VOLUMES

Mack, Merav and Steven Kaplan, eds. *Transnational Christian Communities in the Holy Land.* Special issue of Journal of Levantine Studies 3:1, 2013.

Bowman, Glenn, ed. *Sharing the Sacred: the Politics and Pragmatics of Inter-communal Relations around Holy Places.* New York and Oxford: Berghahn Books, 2012.

Alexander, Paul, ed. *Christ at the Checkpoint: Theology in the Service of Justice and Peace.* Pentecostals, Peacemaking, and Social Justice 4. Allison Park, PA: Pickwick Publications, 2012.

Collings, Rania Al Qass, Rifat Odeh Kassis, and Mitri Raheb, eds. *Palestinian Christians in the West Bank: Facts, Figures and Trends*. Bethlehem: Diyar, 2012.

Mansour, Johnny, ed. *Arab Christians in Israel: Facts, Figures and Trends*. Bethlehem: Diyar, 2012.

Munayer, Salim and Lisa Loden, eds. *The Land Cries Out: Theology of the Land in the Israeli Palestinian Context*. Eugene, OR: Cascade Books, 2012.

Raheb, Mitri, ed. *The Biblical Text in the Context of Occupation: Towards a new hermeneutics of liberation*. Contextual Theology Series 2. Bethlehem: Diyar, 2012.

Reiter, Y. and M. Breger, Leonhard Hammer, eds. *Sacred Space in Israel and Palestine: Religion and Politics*. Routledge Studies in Middle Eastern Politics 41. London: Routledge, 2012.

Raheb, Mitri, ed. *The Invention of History: A Century of Interplay between Theology and Politics in Palestine*. Contextual Theology Series 1. Bethlehem: Diyar, 2011.

Selwyn, Tom. "Tears on the Border: the Case of Rachel's Tomb, Bethlehem, Palestine." In *Contested Mediterranean Spaces: Ethnographic Essays in Honour of Charles Tilly*. Space and Place vol. 4. Edited by Maria Kousis, Tom Selwyn & David Clark. Oxford: Berghahn, 2011.

O'Mahony, Anthony and J. Flannery, eds. *The Catholic Church in the Contemporary Middle East: Studies for the Synod for the Middle East*. London: Melisende, 2010.

Merali, Arzu and Javad Sharbaf, eds. *Towards a New Liberation Theology: Reflections on Palestine*. Wembley: Islamic Human Rights Commission, 2009.

Reiter, Yitzhak, Marshall Breger, and Leonhard Hammer, eds. *Holy Places in the Israeli-Palestinian Conflict: Confrontation and Co-existence*. London: Routledge, 2009.

Rittner, C. and S. D. Smith, eds. *No Going Back: Letters to Pope Benedict XVI on the Holocaust, Jewish-Christian Relations & Israel*. London: Quill Press in Association with the Holocaust Center, 2009.

Ateek, Naim Stifan, Cedar Duaybis, and Maurine Tobin, eds. *The Forgotten Faithful: A Window into the Life and Witness of Christians in the Holy Land*. Jerusalem: Sabeel Ecumenical Liberation Theology Center, 2008.

Brown, Wesley H., and Peter F. Penner, eds. *Christian Perspectives on the Israeli-Palestinian Conflict*. Schwarzenfeld: Neufeld, 2008.

O'Mahony, Anthony, ed. *Christianity in the Middle East: Studies in Modern History, Theology and Politics*. London: Melisende, 2008.

Collings, Rania Al Qass, Rifat Odeh Kassis, and Mitri Raheb, eds. *Palestinian Christians: Facts, Figures and Trends 2008*. Bethlehem: Diyar, 2008.

Sabeel Ecumenical Liberation Theology Center, ed. *The Sabeel Survey on Palestinian Christians in the West Bank and Israel: Historical Demographic Developments, Current Politics and Attitudes Towards Church, Society and Human Rights*. Jerusalem: Sabeel Ecumenical Liberation Theology Center, 2006.

Ateek, Naim Stifan, Cedar Duaybis, and Maurine Tobin, eds. *Challenging Christian Zionism*. London: Melisende, 2005.

Prior, Michael, ed. *Speaking the Truth: Zionism, Israel, and Occupation*. Northhampton, MA: Olive Branch, 2005.

Breger, Marshall J., ed. *The Vatican-Israel Accords: Political, Legal, and Theological Contexts*. Notre Dame: University of Notre Dame Press, 2004.

Hafften, Ann, ed. *Water from the Rock: Lutheran Voices from Palestine*. Minneapolis, MN: Augsburg Fortress 2003.

O'Mahony, Anthony. *The Christian Communities of Jerusalem and the Holy Land: Studies in History, Religion, and Politics.* Cardiff: University of Wales Press, 2003.

Bechmann, Ulrike, and Ottmar Fuchs. *Von Nazareth bis Bethlehem: Hoffnung und Klage Mit einem Forschungsbericht von Saleh Srouji.* Tübinger Perspektiven zur Pastoraltheologie und Religionspädagogik 4. Munster: LIT Verlag, 2002.

Tobin, Maurine and Robert Tobin, eds. *How Long O Lord? Christian, Jewish and Muslim Voices from the Ground and Visions for the Future in Israel/Palestine.* Cambridge, MA: Cowley Publications, 2002.

Suermann, Harald, ed.. *Zwischen Halbmond und Davidstern: christliche Theologie in Palästina heute.* Theologie der Dritten Welt 28. Freiburg: Herder, 2001.

Tamcke, Martin, ed. *Orientalische Christen zwischen Repression und Migration. Beiträge zur jüngeren Geschichte und Gegenwartslage.* Studien zur Orientalischen Kirchengeschichte 13. Munster: LIT Verlag, 2001.

Loden, Lisa, Peter Walker, and Michael Wood, eds. *The Bible and the Land: An Encounter. Different Views: Christian Arab Palestinian, Israeli Messianic Jew, Western Christian.* Jerusalem: Musalaha, 2000.

Swanson, Robert N., ed. *The Holy Land, Holy Lands, and Christian History: Papers Read at the 1998 Summer Meeting and the 1999 Winter Meeting of the Ecclesiastical History Society.* Studies in Church History 36. Oxford: Boydel & Brewer, 2000.

Ateek, Naim Stifan, and Michael Prior, eds. *Holy Land, Hollow Jubilee: God, Justice and the Palestinians.* London: Melisende, 1999.

Ateek, Naim Stifan, and Hilary Rantisi, eds. *"Our Story": The Palestinians.* Jerusalem: Sabeel Ecumenical Liberation Theology Center, 1999.

Carmesund, Ulf, Kevork Hintlian, and Thomas Hummel, eds. *Patterns of the Past, Prospects for the Future: The Christian Heritage in the Holy Land.* London: Melisende, 1999.

O'Mahony, Anthony, ed. *Palestinian Christians: Religion, Politics and Society in the Holy Land.* London: Melisende, 1999.

Pacini, A. ed. *Christian Communities in the Arab Middle East: The Challenge of the Future.* Oxford: Oxford University Press, 1999.

Munayer, Salim, ed. *Seeking and Pursuing Peace: The Process, the Pain, and the Product.* Jerusalem: Musalaha, 1998.

Thordson, Maria, ed. *Christians 2000 A.D.: Men and Women in the Land of Christ, a Living Church History.* London: Minerva Publishing, 1998.

Aghazarian, Albert, Bernard Sabella, Afif Safieh, eds. *Christian Voices from the Holy Land: Out of Jerusalem?* (London?) The Palestinian General Delegation to the United Kingdom, 1997.

Ateek, Naim Stifan, Cedar Duaybis, and Marla Schrader, eds. *Jerusalem: What Makes for Peace! Palestinian Christian Contribution to Peacemaking.* London: Melisende, 1997.

Pax Christi–Deutsches Sekretariat, ed. *Israel/Palästina. Naher Osten—Ferner Frieden?* Schriftenreihe Probleme des Friedens. Politische Schriftenreihe. Idstein: Komzi Verlag, 1997.

Heyer, Friedrich, ed. تاريخ الكنيسة في الارض المقدسة. *(History of the Church in the Holy Land).* Translated by Fahed Abu Ghazali. Bethlehem, 1995.

O'Mahony, Anthony, Göran Gunner, and Kevork Hintlian, eds. *The Christian Heritage in the Holy Land.* London: Scorpion Cavendish, 1995.

Raheb, Mitri and Ulrike Bechmann, eds. *Verwurzelt im Heiligen Land: Einführung in das palästinensische Christentum.* Frankfurt am Main: J. Knecht, 1995.

Munayer, Salim, David Katz, and Benjamin Berger, eds. *Auf den Spuren Abrahams: Juden und Palästinenser versöhnen sich*. With a preface by Roland Werner. Hamburg: GGE-Verlag, 1994.

Prior, Michael, and William Taylor, eds. *Christians in the Holy Land*. London: The World of Islam Festival Trust, 1994.

Ateek, Naim Stifan, Marc H. Ellis, and Rosemary Radford Ruether, eds. *Faith and the Intifada: Palestinian Christian Voices*. Maryknoll, NY: Orbis Books, 1992.

Williamson, Roger, ed. *The Holy Land in the Monotheistic Faiths*. Life & Peace Institute Conference Report 3. Uppsala, 1992.

Bergen, Kathy, David Neuhaus, and Ghassan Rubeiz, eds. *Justice and the Intifada: Palestinians and Israelis Speak Out*. New York: Friendship Press; Geneva: WCC, 1991.

Reuther, Rosemary Radford and Marc Ellis, eds. *Beyond Occupation: American Jewish, Christian and Palestinian Voices for Peace*. Boston: Beacon Press, 1990.

Ecumenical Institute for Theological Research; Al-Liqa' Center for Religious and Heritage Studies in the Holy Land. مؤتمر اللاهوت والكنيسة المحلية في الارض المقدسة. *(Proceedings of the Conference on Theology and the Local Church in the Holy Land)*. Tantur/Jerusalem: The Ecumenical Institute for Theological Research, 1987; Bethlehem/Jerusalem: The Al-Liqa' Center for Religious and Heritage Studies in the Holy Land, 1988–present.

Ecumenical Institute for Theological Research; Al-Liqa' Center for Religious and Heritage Studies in the Holy Land. مؤتمر التراث العربي للمسيحيين والمسلمين في الرض الارض المقدسة. *(Proceedings of the Conference on the Arab Christian and Muslim Traditions in the Holy Land)*. Tantur/Jerusalem: The Ecumenical Institute for Theological Research, 1983–1987; Bethlehem/Jerusalem: The Al-Liqa' Center for Religious and Heritage Studies in the Holy Land, 1988–present.

Ellis, Kail C. *The Vatican, Islam, and the Middle East*. New York, 1987.

Paul Löffler, ed. *Arabische Christen im Nahostkonflikt: Christen im politischen Spannungsfeld*. Frankfurt: Verlag Otto Lembeck, 1976.

ARTICLES OR CHAPTERS IN BOOKS

Dumpter, Michael. "Christianity, Jerusalem and Zionist Exclusivity: the St John's Hospice incident reconsidered." In *Jerusalem Interrupted: Arab Jerusalem and Colonial Transformation 1917 to the Present*. Edited by Lena Jayyusi. Northampton, MA: Olive Branch, 2013.

Bowman, Glenn. "Identification and Identity Formations around Shared Shrines in West Bank Palestine and Western Macedonia." Pages 10–28 in *Sharing Sacred Spaces in the Mediterranean: Christians, Muslims, and Jews at Shrines and Sanctuaries*. Edited by Dionigi Albera and Couroucli Maria. Bloomington: Indiana University Press, 2012.

Bowman, Glenn. "A Place for the Palestinians in the *Altneuland*: Herzl, Anti-Semitism, and the Jewish State." Pages 65–79 in *Surveillance and Control in Israel/Palestine: Population, Territory and Power*. Edited by Elia Zureik, David Lyon and Yasmeen Abu-Laban. New York and London: Routledge, 2010.

Grey, Mary, "Sustaining Hope when Relationality Fails: Reflecting on Palestine—a Case Study." Pages 87–108 in *Through Us, With Us, In Us: Relational Theologies in the 21st Century*. Edited by Lisa Isherwood and Elain Bellchambers. London: SCM, 2010.

Marten, Michael. "Indigenisation and Contextualisation—the Example of Anglican and Presbyterian Churches in the Holy Land." Pages 115–37 in *Christianity and*

Jerusalem: Theology and Politics in the Holy Land. Edited by Anthony O'Mahony. Leominister: Gracewing Publishers, 2010.

Bowman, Glenn. "Israel's Wall and the Logic of Encystation: Sovereign Exception or Wild Sovereignty?" Pages 292–304 in *Crisis of the State: War and Social Upheaval.* Edited by Bruce Kapferer and Bjørn Enge Bertelsen. New York and Oxford: Berghahn Books, 2009.

Younan, Munib. "Beyond Luther: Prophetic Interfaith Dialogue for Life." Pages 49–64 in *The Global Luther: A Theologian for Modern Times.* Edited by Christine Helmer. Minneapolis, MN: Fortress, 2009.

Ramon, Amnon, "הנוצרים בירושלים תחת שלטון ישראל" ("The Christian Churches in Jerusalem under Israeli Rule"). Pages 5–10 in *40 שנה בירושלים (Forty Years in Jerusalem 1967–2007).* Edited by O. Ahimeir and Yaacov Bar-Siman-Tov. Jerusalem: The Jerusalem Institute for Israel Studies, 2008.

Younan, Munib. "The Future of the Lutheran Reformation Tradition: From the Perspective of Palestinian Christians." In *The Future of Lutheranism in a Global Context.* Minneapolis, MN: Augsburg Fortress, 2008.

Smith, David W. and Elizabeth G.B. Smith. "Chapter Ten: Liberation Theologies." Pages 253–76 in *Understanding World Religions: A Road Map for Justice and Peace.* Plymouth: Rowman & Littlefield, 2007.

Seidel, Timothy. "Palestinian Christians: The Forgotten Faithful." Pages 143–52 in *Under Vine and Fig Tree: Biblical Theologies of Land and the Palestinian-Israeli Conflict.* Edited by Alain Epp Weaver. Telford PA: Cascadia Publishing House, 2007.

Weaver, Alain Epp. "Interfaith Bridge Building, Peacebuilding, and Development: Learning from Israel-Palestine." Pages 92–104 in *Boarders and Bridges: Mennonite Witness in a Religiously Diverse World.* Edited by Peter Dula and Alain Epp Weaver. Telford PA: Cascadia Publishing House, 2007.

Bowman, Glenn. "A Death Revisited: Solidarity and Dissonance in a Muslim-Christian Palestinian Community." Pages 27–49 in *Memory and Violence in the Middle East and North Africa.* Edited by Ussama Makdisi and Paul Silverstein. Bloomington: Indiana University Press, 2006.

Gräbe, Uwe. "Mission and Proselytism as a Historical Background to a Contemporary Reformulation of Christian 'Presence and Witness' in the Middle East." Pages 247–55 in *Christian Witness Between Continuity and New Beginnings: Modern Historical Missions in the Middle East.* Studien zur Orientalischen Kirchengeschichte. Edited by Martin Tamcke and Michael Marten. Munster: LIT Verlag, 2006.

Raheb, Viola. "Frieden schaffendes Handeln im Kontext von Krieg: Perspektiven einer Palästinenserin." In *Frauen schaffen Frieden.* Frauen Bibel Arbeiten 17. Düsseldorf: Katholisches Bibelwerk, 2006.

Ramon, Amnon. "The Christian Institutions and the Fence around Jerusalem." Pages 119–36 in *The Security Fence around Jerusalem: Implications for the City and its Residents.* Edited by Israel Kimhi. Jerusalem: The Jerusalem Institute for Israel Studies, 2006.

Younan, Munib. "Theological Reflection and Theology." Pages 17–29 in *Theological Reflection on Accompaniment: A workshop organised by the Ecumenical Accompaniment Programme in Palestine and Israel of The Commission of the Churches on International Affairs in partnership with Faith and Order of the World Council of Churches.* Edited by The World Council of Churches. Geneva: EAPPI Commission of the Churches on International Affairs World Coucnil of Churches, 2005.

Herbert David. "Religion, Conflict and Coexistence in Palestine/Israel." Pages 249–85 in *Religion in history: Conflict, Conversion and Coexistence*. Edited by John Wolffe. Manchester: Manchester University Press, 2004.

Raheb, Viola. "Mit dem Alten Testament im Konflikt um das Land." In *Impuls oder Hindernis? Mit dem Alten Testament in multireligiöser Gesellschaft*. Edited by Joachim Kügler. Berlin: LIT Verlag, 2004.

Raheb, Viola. "I den förlorade barndomens land." In *I sukuggan av ockupationen: palestinsk kamp för nationella rättigheter*. Edited by Göran Gunner. Bokförlaget Atlas, 2004.

Raheb, Viola. "Palästina: Dialog des Lebens." In *Christ sein weltweit: Material für Gemeinden und Gruppen*. Breklum Verlag, 2004.

Raheb, Mitri. "Genom stormigt hav—den palestinka krsitna gemenskapen." In *I Skuggan av Ockupationen—palestinsk kamp för nationella rättigheter*. Edited by Göran Gunner. Stockholm: Bokförlaget Atlas, 2004.

Raheb, Mitri. "Tvivlrådige, men ikke fortvivlede." In *Årbog 2003–2004: Kirkir I Mellemøsten*. Frederiksberg, Denmark: De mellemkirkelige Råd, 2004.

Roussos, Sotiris. "Patriarchs, Notables and Diplomats: the Greek Orthodox Patriarchate of Jerusalem in the Modern Period." Pages 372–87 in *Eastern Christianity: Studies in Modern History, Religion and Politics*. Edited by Anthony O'Mahony. London: Melisende, 2004.

Raheb, Mitri. "Facing Antisemitism and Anti-Judaism Today: Country Reports—Palestine." Pages 157–58 in *A Shift in Jewish-Lutheran Relations?* Edited byWolfgang Greive and Peter N. Prove. LWF Documentation No. 48. The Lutheran World Federation: Geneva, 2003.

Raheb, Mitri. "Der Islam: Ein gescheitertes oder gelungenes Projekt christlich-arabischer Kontextualisierung?" Pages 281–318 in *Jenseits der Festungsmauern*. Edited by Ulrich Dehn and Klaus Hock. Neuendettelsau: Erlanger Verlag fuer Mission und Oekumene, 2003.

Raheb, Viola. "Women in Contemporary Palestinian Society: A Contextual Reading of the Book of Ruth." In *Feminist Interpretation of the Bible and the Hermeneutics of Liberation*. Edited by Silvia Schroer and Sophia Bietenhard. Sheffield: Sheffield Academic Press, 2003.

Raheb, Viola. "Die Landnahme- ein Stolperstein für meinen Glauben?" In *Bitte Stolpern! Provozierende Texte der Bibel*. Edited by Dieter Bauer, Sabine Bieberstein and Angelika Boesch. Bibelwerk, 2003.

Raheb, Viola, and Anneliese Hecht. "Ich sah die heilige Stadt, das neue Jerusalem. Bibelarbeit zu Offb. 21." In *Frauen Sehnsucht*. Frauen Bibel Arbeiten 11. Edited by Hedwig Lamberty-Zielinsky. Düsseldorf, 2003.

Raheb, Viola. "Die Kreuzigung Bethlehems." In *Israel/ Palästina: Wenn aus Opfer Täter werden. Berichte, Gespräche, Begegnungen*. Edited by Dolores M. Bauer. Klosterneuburg: Edition VA Bene, 2002.

Tsimhoni, Daphne. "The Christians in Israel: Aspects of Integration and the Search for Identity in a Minority within a Minority." Pages 124–52 in *Middle Eastern Minorities and Diasporas*. Edited by Moshe Ma'oz and Gabriel Sheffer. Tel Aviv: Sussex Academic Press, 2002.

Raheb, Viola. "Bildung ist ein Weg zur Veränderung": Die Schularbeit der Evangelisch Lutherischen Kirche in Jordanien." In *Seht, wir gehen hinauf nach Jerusalem: Festschrift zum 150 Jährigen Jubiläum von Taltha Kumi und des Jerusalemsvereins.*

Edited by Almut Nothnagle, Hans-Jürgen Abromeit, and Frank Foerste. Leipzig: Evangelische Verlags-Anstalt, 2001.

Raheb, Viola. "Religiös-politische Indoktrination oder tolerant gelebter Glaube als Grundlage der Erziehung: das Spannungsfeld bei religiös getragenen Schulen im Nahen Osten." In *Spiritualität und ethische Erziehung: Erbe und Herausforderung der Religionen*. Pädagogische Beiträge zur Kulturbegegnung 20. Berlin: EB-Verlag 2001.

Ateek, Naim Stifan. "Zionism and the Land: A Palestinian Christian Perspective." Pages 201–14 in *The Land of Promise: Biblical Theological and Contemporary Perspectives*. Edited by Philip Johnston and Peter Walker. Downers Grove, IL: Apollos, 2000.

Uriely, Natan, Aviad Israeli, and Arie Reichel. "Residents' Attitudes toward Tourism Events: The Case of Nazareth 2000." Pages 99–115 in *Proceedings of the Second International Seminar on Tourism Management in Heritage Cities. Nazareth, 3–5 February 2000*. Edited by Antonio Paolo Russo. Technical Report 30. Venice: UNESCO Venice Office, 2000.

Bechmann, Ulrike. "Palästinensische Christen und Christinnen: die unbequeme Seite des christlich-jüdischen Dialogs." Pages 169–79 in *Mich erinnern—dich erkennen—uns erleben: 50 Jahre Gesellschaft für christlich-jüdische Zusammenarbeit in Frankfurt am Main 1949–1999*. Edited by Gesellschaft für christlich-jüdische Zusammenarbeit in Frankfurt/Main. Frankfurt, 1999.

Mavrides, C. "The Diaries of Constantine Mavrides (May 15—December 30, 1948)." In *Jerusalem 1948: The Arab Neighbourhoods and Their Fate in the War*. Edited by S. Tamari. Institute for Palestine Studies, 1999.

Raheb, Mitri. "Die Bibel aus der Perspektive eines palästinensischen Christen." In *Wirkungen: Der Umgang derBibel im Wandel der Zeiten*. Reihe Brennpunkt: Die Bibel. With a preface by Joachim Rogge. Erfurt: Evangelische Haupt-Bibelgesellschaft and Cansteinsche Bibelanstalt, 1999.

Raheb, Viola. "Sehnsucht nach Heimat." In *Von der Sehnsucht: Entwürfe*. Edited by Norbert Sommer. Berlin: Wichern Verlag, 1999.

Ramon, Amnon. "Freedom of Religion and the Status of the Christians in Jerusalem 1967–1997." in *Freedom of Religion in Jerusalem*. Edited by O. Ahimeir and R. Lapidoth. Jerusalem: The Jerusalem Institute for Israel Studies, 1999.

Roussos, Sotiris. "The Greek Orthodox Community of Jerusalem in International Politics: International Solutions for Jerusalem and the Greek Orthodox Community in the Nineteenth and Twentieth Centuries." Pages 482–93 in *Jerusalem: Its Sanctity and Centrality to Judaism, Christianity, and Islam*. Edited by Lee I. Levine. New York: Continuum, 1999.

Suermann, Harald. "Neuere Veröffentlichungen zur palästinensischen Theologie." Pages 206–28 in *Jahrbuch für Kontextuelle Theologien* 99. Edited by Missionswissenschaftliches Institut missio e.V. Frankfurt am Main, 1999.

Sabella, Bernard. "The Emigration of Christian Arabs: Dimensions and Causes of the Phenomenon." In *Christian Communities in the Arab Middle East, the Challenge for the Future*. Edited by Andrea Pacini. Oxford: Clarendon, 1998.

Tsimhoni, Daphne. "Palestinian Christians and the Peace Process: The Dilemma of a Minority." Pages 141–60 in *The Middle East Peace Process: Interdisciplinary Perspectives*. Edited by Ilan Peleg. New York: State University of New York, 1998.

Tsimhoni, Daphne. "הנוצרים בישראל: בין דת לפוליטיקה" ("Christians in Israel: Between Religion and Politics"). Pages 139–64 in *The Arabs in Israeli Politics: Dilemmas of Identity*. Edited by Elie Rekhess. Tel Aviv: Tel Aviv University, 1998.

Stöhr, Martin. "Jüdisch-christlicher Dialog und palästinensische Theologie: Ein notwendiger Streit in der Ökumene." Pages 156–70 in *Dreinreden: Essays, Vorträge, Thesen, Meditationen*. Edited by Klaus Müller und Alfred Wittstock, Wuppertal: Foedus, 1997.

Raheb, Mitri. "Christlich-islamischer Dialog in Palästina." Pages 8–11 in *CIBEDO: Beiträge zum Gespräch zwischen Christen und Muslimen*. Edited by Deutsche Provinz der Weißen Väter (10. Jahrgang, Nr. 1) 1996.

Raheb, Mitri. "Lutherisches Zeugnisin Israel/Palaestina." Pages 36–9 in *Lutherisches Bekenntnis in ökumenischer Verpflichtung (Arbeitsheft mit Texten von der Generalsynode der VELKD in Lüneburg vom 19. bis 23. Oktober 1996)*. Edited by Lutherisches Kirchenamt der VELKD. 1996.

Raheb, Mitri. "Fundamentalismus im Islam: Demokratie im Nahen Osten." Pages 201–6 in *Fundamentalismus der Moderne? Christen und Muslime im Dialog*. Loccumer Protokolle 57/94. Edited by Sybille Fritsch-Oppermann. Evang. Akad. Loccum, 1996.

Raheb, Mitri. "The Diverse Communities in Israeli and Palestinian Societies." Pages 51–7 in *Religion and State in Israeli and Palestinian Society*. Edited by Natasha Dudinski. Jerusalem: IPCRI Civil Society Publications, 1996.

Sabbah, Michel. "Jerusalem steht niemandem alleine zu: Palästinenser und Isrealis werden gemeinsam eine Lösung finden." Pages 265–88 in *Die Jerusalem Frage: Israelis und Palästinenser im Gespräch*. Edited by Uri Avneri and Azmi Bishara. Heidelberg, 1996.

Ateek, Naim Stifan. "Pentecost and the Intifada." Pages 69–81 in *Reading from this Place, vol. 2: Social Location and Biblical. Interpretation in Global Perspective*. Edited by F. F. Segovia and M. Tolbert. Minneapolis, MN: Fortress, 1995.

Ateek, Naim, "Jerusalem in Islam and for Palestinian Christians," Pages 128–9 in *Jerusalem Past and Present in the Purposes of God*. Edited by Peter Walker. Grand Rapids: Baker, 1994.

Raheb, Mitri. "Jericho zuerst." Pages 174–9 in *Für Gerechtigkeit streiten. Theologie im Alltag einer bedrohten Welt. Festschrift für Luise Schottroff zum 60. Geburtstag*. Edited by Dorothee Sölle. Gütersloh, Gütersloher Verlagshaus, 1994.

Suermann, Harald. "Kultur und Kircheneinheit im Nahen Osten." Pages 87–99 in *Inkulturation und Kontextualität: Theologien im weltweiten Austausch. Festgabe für Ludwig Bertsch SJ zum 65. Geburtstag*. Edited by Pankoke-Schenk and Evers. Fankfurt: Josef Knecht, 1994.

Khoury, Geries Sa'ed. "Olive Tree Theology—Rooted in the Palestinian Soil." Pages 38–75 in *Jahrbuch für kontextuelle Theologien—Yearbook of Contextual Theologies* 93. Edited by Missionswissenschaftliches Institut Missio e.V. Aachen, 1993.

Pedersen, Kirsten Stoffregen. "Ethiopian Iconography in Jerusalem 1970–1990." Pages 141–4 in *Aspects of Ethiopian Art from Ancient Axum to the 20th Century*. Edited by Paul B. Henze. London: The Jed Press, 1993. Evangelische

Raheb, Mitri. "Biblical Interpretation in the Israeli-Palestinian Context." Pages 109–17 in *Israel and Yeshua (Caspari Center for Biblical and Jewish Studies)*. Edited by Torleif Elgvin. Jerusalem, 1993.

Raheb, Mitri, and Karl-Heinz Roneck, "Der israelisch-palästinensische Konflikt und das Zeugnis der Christen." Pages 122–34 in *Erkunden und Versöhnen. Ökumenisches Arbeitsbuch Heinz Joachim Held zu Ehren*. Beiheft zur Oekumenischen Rundschau 65. Edited by Hans Vorster and Hermann Göckenjan. Frankfurt am M.: Verlag Otto Lambeck, 1993.

Rubenson, Samuel. "Church and State, Communion and Community: Some issues in the recent ecclesiastical history of Jerusalem." Pages 84–102 in *The Middle East Unity and Diversity*. Nordic Proceedings in Asian Studies 5. Edited by Heikki Palva and Knut S. Vikor. Copenhagen: Nias Press, 1993.

Bowman, Glenn. "The politics of tour guiding: Israeli and Palestinian guides in Israel and the Occupied Territories." Pages 121–34 in *Tourism and the Less Developed Countries*. Edited by David Harrison. London: Belhaven Press.

Du Brul, Fr. Peter. "Crisis of Palestinian Christians." In *Voices from Jerusalem: Jews and Christians reflect on the Holy Land*. Studies in Judaism and Christianity. Edited by David B. Burrell and Yehezkel Landau. New York: Paulist, 1992.

Ellis, Marc H. "Beyond the ecumenical dialogue: Jews, Christians and the challenge of the Palestinian people." In *A Mutual Witness: Toward Critical Solidarity between Jews and Christians*. Edited by Clark M. Williamson. St. Louis, MO: Chalice, 1992.

Tsimhoni, Daphne. "The Latin Patriarchate of Jerusalem from the First Half of the 19th Century to Present Times: Institutional and Social Aspects." In *The Arabs in Jerusalem: From the Late Ottoman Period to the Beginning of the 1990s—Relgious, Social and Cultural Distinctiveness*. Hamizrah Hehadash, Vol. XXXIV. Jerusalem, 1992.

Cragg, Kenneth, "Chapter 10: Arab Christianity and Israel." Pages 233–56 in *The Arab Christian: A History in the Middle East*. Louisville: Westminster/John Knox, 1991.

Khoury, Geries Sa'ed. "The Role of Religion in Conflict Situation: Palestinian Perspective." Pages 79–86 in *Consultation: The Role of Religion in Conflict Situation*. Edited by The Middle East Council of Churches. Beirut-Cyprus, 1991.

Krupp, Michael. "Situation der Christen in Israel und in den besetzten Gebieten." Pages 101–6 in *40 Jahre Staat Israel 1948/1988: Eine Arbeitshilfe für Unterricht, Fortbildung und Gemeindearbeit*. Edited by Evangelischer Arbeitskreis Kirche und Israel in Hessen und Nassau. Heppenheim: Ev. AK Kirche, 1988.

Khoury, F.J. "The Jerusalem Question and the Vatican." Pages 143–62 in *The Vatican, Islam and the Middle East*. Edited by H.F. Ellis. New York: Syracuse University Press, 1987.

Samir, S. Khalil. "La tradition arabe chrétienne et la chrétienté de Terre-Sainte." Pages 343–432 in *Tantur Papers on Christianity in the Holy Land*. Edited by David M. Jaeger. Studia Oecumenica Hierosolymitana 1. Jerusalem: Tantur, 1981.

Sim'an, Ibrahim. "Issues Facing the Arab Christian Today." Pages 24–8 in *Let Jews and Arabs Hear His Voice: Christian Life and Ministry in the Encounter with Jews and Arabs in Israel Today*. Edited by Ole C. M. Kvarme. Ten papers presented by the United Christian Council in Israel. Jerusalem: The United Christian Council in Israel, 1981.

Tsimhoni, Daphne. "The Arab Christians and the Palestinian Arab National Movement during the Formative Stage." Pages 73–98 in *The Palestinians and the Middle East Conflict*. Edited by Gabriel Ben-Gor. Ramat Gan: Universtiy of Haifa, 1978.

Sakhnini, Fouad. "The Gospel and Arab Thinking." Pages 135–40 in *Prophecy in the Making: Messages Prepared for Jerusalem Conference on Biblical Prophecy*. Edited by Carl Henry. Carol Stream: Creation House, 1971.

JOURNAL ARTICLES

Bowman, Glenn. "Popular Palestinian Practices around Holy Places and Those Who Oppose Them: An Historical Introduction." *Religion Compass* 7 (2013) 69–78.

Bowman, Glenn. "A Weeping on the Road to Bethlehem: Contestation over the Uses of Rachel's Tomb." *Religion Compass* 7 (2013) 79–92.

Kaartveit, Baard Helge. "The Christians of Palestine: Strength, Vulnerability, and Self-restraint within a Multi-sectarian Community." *Middle Eastern Studies* 49:5 (2013) 732–49.

Schmid, Muriel. "From the Church of the Nativity to the Churches of the World: Palestinian Christians and Their 'Cry of Hope.'" *Theology Today* 69:4 (2013) 428–40.

Daoud, Abu. "Reflections on a Palestinian Sojourn: *Christ at the Checkpoint* 2012, Bethlehem, West Bank." *St Francis Magazine* 8:2 (2012) 271–82.

Fretheim, Kjetil. "The Power of Invitation: The Moral Discourse of Kairos Palestine." *Dialog* 51:2 (2012) 135–44.

Kuruvilla, Samuel J. "Palestinian theological praxis in context: Peacemaking and peacebuilding in the Occupied West Bank." *Gandhi Marg: Quarterly Journal of the Gandhi Peace Foundation* 34:1 (2012) 33–50.

Madanat, Hanan and Imad Twal. " 'Communion and Witness': the Contribution of Latin Patriarchate Schools to better Muslim-Christian relations in the Holy Land." *International Studies in Catholic Education* 4 (2012) 35–49.

Masalha, Nur. "Naji Al-Ali, Edward Said and Civil Liberation Theology in Palestine: Contextual, Indigenous and Decolonising Methodologies." *Holy Land Studies* 11:2 (2012)109–34.

Miller, Duane Alexander. "Christ Church (Anglican) in Nazareth: a brief history with photographs." *St Francis Magazine* 8:5 (2012) 696–703.

Miller, Duane Alexander. "The First Church of the Diocese of Jerusalem: A Work in Progress? The Third Sunday of Advent, 11 December 2011." *Anglican and Episcopal History* 81:2 (2012).

Preda, Radu. "Occupation as Sin." *The Ecumenical Review* 64:1 (2012) 7–13.

Ventura, Jonathan. "Conflict and Strife on the way to Gethsemane." *Israel Affairs* 18 (2012) 234–49.

Bowman, Glenn. "In dubious Battle on the Plains of Heav'n': the Politics of Possession in Jerusalem's Holy Sepulchre." *History and Anthropology* 22 (2011) 371–99.

Frantzman, Seth J., Benjamin W. Glueckstadt, and Ruth Kark. "The Anglican Church in Palestine and Israel: Colonialism, Arabization and Land Ownership." *Middle Eastern Studies* 47:1 (2011) 101–26.

Feldman, Jackie. "Abraham the Settler, Jesus the Refugee: Contemporary Conflict and Christianity on the Road to Bethlehem." *History & Memory* 23 (2011) 62–95.

Fernandes, AT, R. Gonçalves, S. Gomes, D. Filon, A. Nebel, M. Faerman, and A. Brehm. "Y-chromosomal STRs in two populations from Israel and the Palestinian Authority Area: Christian and Muslim Arabs." *Forensic Science International. Genetics* 5 (2011) 561–2.

Koulouri, Anna. "The Greek Orthodox Church and the Future of Jerusalem." *Palestine-Israel Journal of Politics, Economics & Culture* 17 (2011) 230–6.

Kuruvilla, Samuel J. "Palestinian Christian Politics in Comparative Perspective: The Case of Jerusalem's Churches and the Indigenous Arab Christians." *Holy Land Studies: A Multidisciplinary Journal (Edinburgh University Press)* 10 (2011) 199–228.

Robson, Laura. "Communalism and Nationalism in the Mandate: The Greek Orthodox Controversy and the National Movement." *Journal of Palestine Studies* 41 (2011) 6–23.

Suleiman, J. and B. Mohamed. "Factors Impact on Religious Tourism Market: The Case of the Palestinian Territories." *International Journal of Business and Management* 6 (2011) 254–60.

Ventura, Jonathan. "Under the Flag of Blue and White: Mary as an A-National Symbol in the Greek-Orthodox Community in Israel." *Sociology Mind* 1 (2011) 230–8.

Bowman, Glenn. "Networks Disrupted: A Study of the Impact of Walling on Contiguous Communities in Israel/Palestine." *Bulletin of the Council for British Research in the Levant* 5 (2010) 85–9.

Greenham, Anthony. "A Study of Palestinian Muslim Converts to Christ." *St Francis Magazine 6:1* (2010) 116–75.

Katanacho, Yohanna. "المصطلح "عرب" في العهد القديم." ("The Term 'Arab' in the Old Testament'). رابطة الشرق الأوسط لمتعميم الالهوتي 5 (2010) 1–11.

Khoury, Rafiq and Paul Duvignau. "Une nouvelle bienheureuse palestinienne: Mère Marie-Alphonsine Ghattas (1843–1927)." *Revue Proche-Orient Chrétien* 60:1–2 (2010) 65–77.

Lewy, M. "Pope Benedict XVI within the Context of Israel and the Holy See Relations." *Israel Affairs* 16 (2010) 562–78.

Robson, Laura. "Palestinian liberation theology, Muslim-Christian relations and the Arab-Israeli conflict." *Islam and Christian-Muslim Relations* 21:1 (2010) 39–50.

Sharaby, Rachel. "Bridge over the Wadi: a Festival of Coexistence in Israel." *Middle Eastern Studies* 46 (2010) 117–30.

Bishara, Amahl. "Palestinian Christian Networked Activism: Reifying 'Nonviolence' or Divining Justice?" *Review of Middle East Studies* 43 (2009) 178–88.

Bush, Andrew F. "The Implications of Christian Zionism for Mission." *International Bulletin of Missionary Research* 33 (2009) 144–51.

Farah, Fuad. "Orthodox Christianity in the Holy Land." *Studies in World Christianity* 15 (2009) 248–58.

Marsh, Leonard. "Whose Holy Land?" *Studies in World Christianity* 15 (2009) 276–86.

Morin, Gabriel. "Brève chronique du pèlerinage du pape Benoît XVI en Terre Sainte." *Revue Proche-Orient Chrétien* 59: 3–4 (2009) 269–94.

Ricks, Thomas M. "Khalil Totah: the Unknown Years." *Jerusalem Quarterly (Institute of Palestine Studies)* 34 (2009) 51–77.

Rjoob, Ahmed. "The Impact of Israeli Occupation on the Conservation of Cultural Heritage Sites in the Occupied Palestinian Territories: The Case of 'Salvage Excavations' ." *Conservation and Management of Archaeological Sites* 11 (2009) 214–35.

Katanacho, Yohanna. "Hagar from a Palestinian Arab Evangelical Perspective." *Roundtable* (2008) 55–9.

Katanacho, Yohanna. "Palestinian Protestant Theological Responses to a World Marked by Violence." *Missiology: An International Review* 36:3 (2008).

Jeppesen, Knud. "Justice with mercy: About a contemporary Palestinian theology." *Hervormde Teologiese Studies* 4:1 (2008) 195–206.

Munayer, Salim J. "The Theological Challenge the State of Israel Poses to Palestinian Christians." *St Francis Magazine* 4:3 (2008) 1–5.

Sharaby, Rachel, "The Holiday of Holidays: a Triple-Holiday Festival for Christians, Jews and Muslims." *Social Compass: International Review of Sociology of Religion* 55 (2008) 581–596.

Bowman, Glenn. "Viewing the Holy City: An Anthropological Perspectivalism." *Jerusalem Quarterly* 31 (2007) 27–39.

Lybarger, L.D. "For Church or Nation? Islamism, Secular-Nationalism, and the Transformation of Christian Identities in Palestine." *American Academy of Religion. Journal of the American Academy of Religion* 75:4 (2007) 777–813.

Ata, Abe. "The Hard Life of Christians in Bethlehem." *Eureka Street* 17:23 (2007) 25–6.

Younan, Munib, "The Future of Palestinian Christianity and Prospects for Justice, Peace, and Reconciliation." *Currents in Theology and Mission* 34 (2007) 338–50.

Epp Weaver, Alain. "Further footnotes on Zionism, Yoder, and Boyarin," *Cross Currents* (Winter, 2007) n.p.

Horenczyk, G. and S.J. Munayer. "Acculturation Orientations Toward Two Majority Groups: The Case of Palestinian Arab Christian Adolescents in Israel." *Journal of Cross-Cultural Psychology* 38:1 (2007) 76–86.

Karayanni, M. "Multiculture Me No More! On Multicultural Qualifications and the Palestinian-Arab Minority of Israel." *Diogenes* 54 (2007) 39–58.

Katanacho, Yohanna. "Allah and the Messenger of Allah in the Book of Malachi." *MennoLetter* 6 (2007) 5–6.

Katz, Itamar and Ruth Kark. "The Church and Landed Property: The Greek Orthodox Patriarchate of Jerusalem." *Middle Eastern Studies* 43 (2007) 383–408.

Khoury, Rafiq. "Les chrétiens de Terre Sainte: experience historique et réalité présente." *Revue Proche-Orient Chrétien* 57: 3–4 (2007) 291–317.

Maier, Thomas. "L'Église arménienne de Jérusalem: histoire et actualité." *Revue Proche-Orient Chrétien* 57: 1–2 (2007) 58–76.

Miller, Duane Alexander. "Morning Prayer, Low Style, in the Anglican Diocese of Jerusalem: Church of the Redeemer." *Anglican and Episcopal History* 76 (2007) 404–8.

Miller, Duane Alexander. "The Installation of a Bishop in Jerusalem: The Cathedral Church of St. George the Martyr." *Anglican and Episcopal History* 76 (2007) 549–554.

McCallum, F. "The Political Role of the Patriarch in the Contemporary Middle East." *Middle Eastern Studies* 43 (2007) 923–40.

Radai, I. "The Collapse of the Palestinian-Arab Middle Class in 1948: The Case of Qatamon." *Middle East Studies* 43 (2007).

Miller, Charles H. "Hermeneutical Problems for a Palestinian Catholic Reading the Old Testament and Current Pastoral Responses." *Aram* 18 (2006) 229–305.

Karayanni, M. "Living in a Group of One's Own: Negative Implications Related to the Private Nature of the Religious Accommodations for the Palestinian-Arab Minorities in Israel." *UCLA Journal of Islamic and Near Eastern Law* 6:1 (2005) 1–45.

O'Mahony, Anthony. "Christian Presence, Church-State Relations and Theology in Modern Jerusalem: The Holy See, Palestinian Christianity and the Latin Patriarchate of Jerusalem in the Holy Land." *Aram* 18 (2006) 229–305.

O'Mahony, Anthony. "Christian Presence in Modern Jerusalem: Religion and Politics in the Holy Land." *Evangelical Quarterly* 78 (2006) 257–72.

Zang, J. "The Forgotten Christians in the Holy Land: An Example of Ecumenism in Everyday Life." *Schneller: Magazine on Christian Life in the Middle East* 121:1 (2006).

Awad, Alex. "Christian Zionism: Their Theology, Our Nightmare!" *MCC Peace Office Newsletter* 35/3 (2005) 2–4.

Bialer, U. "Horse Trading: Israel and the Greek Orthodox Ecclesiastical Property, 1948–52." *The Journal of Israeli History* 24 (2005) 203–13.

Cohen, Michelle. "States of Witness: An Anthropological Perspective on Palestinian Christian Nationalisms." *Koinonia* 17 (2005) 31–40.

Ehrlich, A. "The Developing Attitudes of Arab Christianity towards the State of Israel." *Parole de l'Orient* 30 (2005) 481–531.

Frisch, Hillel. "Israel and its Arab Citizens." *Israel Affairs* 11:1 (2005) 207

Katanacho, Yohanna. "Christ Is the Owner of Haaretz." *Christian Scholar's Review* 34 (2005) 425–41.

Katz, Itamar and Ruth Kark. "The Greek Orthodox Patriarchate of Jerusalem and Its Congregation: Dissent over Real Estate." *International Journal of Middle East Studies* 37:4 (2005) 509–34.

Khawaja, Irfan. " 'Palestinian Christians and Nationalism(s)': Religious Resources for Conflict-Resolution?" *Koinonia* 17 (2005) 45–9.

Marsh, Leonard. "Palestinian Christianit—A Study in Religion and Politics." *International Journal for the Study of the Christian Church* 5:2 (2005) 147–66.

O'Mahony, Anthony. "Christianity and Jerusalem: Religion, Politics and Theology in the Modern Holy Land." *International Journal for the Study of the Christian Church* 5:2 (2005) 86–102.

O'Mahony, Anthony. "The Vatican, Jerusalem, the State of Israel, and Christianity in the Holy Land." *International journal for the Study of the Christian Church* 5:2 (2005) 123–46.

O'Mahony, Anthony, "Rome and Jerusalem: the Vatican and Christianity in the Holy Land." *Bulletin of the Royal Institute for Inter-Faith Studies* 7 (2005) 99–139.

Smith, Robert O., "Palestinian Christians and Nationalism(s) Religious and Secular." *Koinonia* 17 (2005) 1–30.

Stratton, Lawrence M. "Pernicious Prophecy." *Koinonia* 17 (2005) 57–63.

Smith, Robert O. "Secular and Religious: ELCJHL Contributions to Palestinian Nationalism." *Currents in Theology and Mission* 32 (2005) 338–47.

Racionzer, Leon Menzies. "Christianity in Modern Israel." *International Journal for the Study of the Christian Church* 5:2 (2005) 167–81.

Racionzer, Leon Menzies. "Christianity in Modern Israel." *International Journal for the Study of the Christian Church* 5 (2005) 147–66.

Roussos, Sotiris. "Eastern Orthodox Perspectives on Church-State Relations and Religion and Politics in Modern Jerusalem." *International journal for the Study of the Christian Church* 5:2 (2005) 103–22.

Saliba, Sarsar. "Palestinian Christians: Religion, Conflict and the Struggle for Just Peace." *Holy Land Studies* 4 (2005) 27–50.

Weiner, Justus Reid. "Palestinian Christians: Equal Citizens or Oppressed Minority in a Future Palestinian State?" *Oregon Review of International Law* 7 (2005) 26.

Grafton, David D. "The Use of Scripture in the Current Israeli-Palestinian Conflict." *Word & World* 24:1 (2004) 29–39.

Khoury, Rafiq. "The Christian Religious Education in the Schools of the Palestinian Authority." *Proche-Orient Chrétien* 54 (2004) 313–19.

Maier, Thomas. "The Syrian Orthodox Church in Jerusalem. A view on its history and presence in the Holy Land." *Proche-Orient Chrétien* 54 (2004) 305–12.

Suermann, Harald. "Rafiq Khoury: Theologe aus Palästina." *Forum Weltkirche: Zeitschrift für Kirche und Gesellschaft mit weltweitem Blick* 1 (2004), n.p.

Bowman, Glenn. "Constitutive Violence and the Nationalist Imaginary: Antagonism and Defensive Solidarity in 'Palestine' and 'Former Yugoslavia.'" *Social Anthropology* 11 (2003) 319–40.

Eordegian, M. "British and Israeli Maintenance of the Status Quo in the Holy Places of Christendom." *International Journal of Middle East Studies* 35 (2003) 307–28.

Epp Weaver, Alain. "Yoder, Said, and a Theology of Land and Return," *CrossCurrents* (Winter, 2003) n.p.

Leeming, Kate. "The Adoption of Arabic as a Liturgical Language by the Palestinian Melkite." *Aram* 15 (2003) 239–46.

Stricker, Gerd. "Russische Klöster im Heiligen Land." *Journal of Eastern Christian Studies* 55:1–2 (2003) 47–64.

Bowman, Glenn. " 'Migrant Labour': Constructing Homeland in the Exilic Imagination." *Anthropological Theory* 2 (2002) 447–68.

Dumper, Michael, "The Christian Churches of Jerusalem in the Post-Oslo Period", *Journal of Palestine Studies* 31 (2002) 51–65.

Raheb, Mitri. "Sailing Through Troubled Waters: Palestinian Christians in the Holy Land." *Dialog* 41:2 (2002) 97–102.

Raheb, Viola. "Frauen räumen das Feld: Das Engagement für Frieden vieler Frauen bleibt unsichtbar." *an.schläge: Das feministische Magazin* 11 (2002) 14–23.

Reitsma, BJG. "Who is our God? The Theological Challenges of the State of Israel for Christian Arabs. Faith and Ethnicity in the Middle East." *Studies in Reformed Theology* (2002).

Bowman, Glenn. "The Two Deaths of Basem Rishmawi: Identity Constructions and Reconstructions in a Muslim-Christian Palestinian Community." *Identities* 8 (2001) 47–81.

Katanacho, Yohanna. "성지의 팔레스틴 그리스도인들" ("Palestinian Christians in the Holy Land") 민중과신학6 (2001) 52–65

Khoury, Rafiq. "Un peuple en Palestine." *Ceras-Projet: Recherche et Action sociales* 267 (2001) : 24–31.

Laird, Lance D. "Meeting Jesus Again in the First Place: Palestinian Christians and the Bible." *Interpretation* 55:4 (2001) 401–12.

Munayer, Salim. "On the Road to Reconciliation." *Mishkan* 35 (2001) 32–40.

Tsimhoni, Daphne. "The Christians in Israel and the Territories—Disappearance." *Middle East Quarterly (Rutgers University)* 8 (2001) 31–42.

Abou Ramadan, Moussa. "The Law Applicable to the Rum Orthodox Minority in the State of Israel." *Proche-Orient Chrétien* 50 (2000) 105–41.

Abdul-Masih, Margeurite. "The Challenge of Present-Day Palestine to Contemporary Theology." *Studies in Religion/Sciences Religieuses* 29:4 (2000) 439–51.

Usher, Graham. "Seeking sanctuary: the 'Church' vs. 'Mosque' dispute in Nazareth." *Middle East Report* 214/30 (2000) 2–4.

Weiner, Justus. "The False Prophet of Palestine: In the Wake of the Edward Said Revelations." *Jerusalem Letter/Viewpoints* 422 (2000) n.p.

Raheb, Viola. "Frauen in der Palästinensischen Gesellschaft heute." *Bibel und Kirche* 54:3 (1999).

Gräbe, Uwe. "Herausforerung des Jubeljahres: Was fordert Gott?" *Palästina Journal* 35 (1998) 20.

Raheb, Viola. "Bildung als Herausforderung." *Palästina Verstehen* 40 (1998).

Ruether, Rosemary Radford. "Auf palästinensische Christen hören: Eine Herausforderung an die biblische Tradition." *Reformatio* 37 (1998) 422–28.

Fuchs, Ottmar. "Ortsbegehung palästinensischer Erfahrungen und Theologie." *Pastoraltheologische Informationen* 17 (1997) 79–98.

Raheb, Mitri. "Mission in the context of Fragmentation." *International Review of Mission* 86:343 (1997) 393–98.

Raheb, Mitri. "Contextualising the Scripture: Towards a New Understanding of the Qur'an in Arab-Christian Perspective." *Studies in World Christianity* 3/2 (1997) 180–201.

Bechmann, Ulrike. "Vom Dialog zur Solidarität: Entwicklungen im arabischen christlich-islamischen Dialog in Palästina." *CIBEDO Beiträge zum Gespräch zwischen Christen und Muslimen* 11 (1997) 61–6.

El-Assal, Riach Abu, and Samir Kafeety. " Stellungnahme der Kirchenleitung der Bischöflichen Kirche in Jerusalem und dem Mittleren Osten zur gegenwärtigen Lage in Israel/Palästina Anfang Oktober 1996." *EMS Informationsbrief* 1 (1997) 28.

Grübe, Uwe. "Palästinenser und Israeli im muslimisch-christlich-jüdischen Dialog." *Evangelische Zeitung: Wochenzeitung für die Landeskirchen Braunschweig, Hannover und Oldenburg* 5 (1997) 10.

Naber, Gerhard. " 'Die Bibel mit den Augen eines Palästinensers lessen . . .': Eine Annäherung an die Palästinensiche Befreiungstheologie." *Reformierte Kirchenzeitung* 9 (1997) 390–94.

Raheb, Mitri. "Religion und Politik in Palästina: Muslime, Christen und Juden." *EMS Informationsbrief* 1 (1997) 12–15.

Raheb, Viola. "Jugendliche, Kinder: ihre Rolle in Palästina." *EMS Informationsbrief* 1 (1997) 16–20.

Raheb, Viola. "Brennende Kerzen gegen die Angst: Das Internationale Begegnungszentrum in Bethlehem." *Darum: Zeitschrift des Evangelischen Missionswerkes in Südwestdeutschland e.V., für die Freunde des Missionswerkes* 6 (1997) 18–9.

Ariel, Yaakov. "Born Again in a Land of Paradox: Christian Fundamentalists in Israel." *Fides et Historia* 28 (1996) 35–49.

Goetze, Andreas. "Israel in der Theologie christlicher Palästinenser." *Deutsches Pfaffrerblatt* 2 (1996) 62–5.

Sabbah, Michel. "Les Chrétiens de Terre Sainte aujourd'hui et le dialogue des religions." *Courrier Œcuménique* 28 (1996) : 50–57.

Sabella, Bernard. "The Vocation of Jerusalem: A Christian Perspective." *Current Dialogue 30* (1996)

Schneider, Thomas. "Palästinensische Christen: 'Hierbleiben ist die Hauptsache'. Warum die junge Generation auswandert, und was die kirchliche Jugendarbeit dagegen tut." *Publik Forum* 16 (1996) 32.

Raheb, Mitri. "Christlich-muslimischer Dialog in Palästina." *Palästina Journal* 27 (1996) 3–6.

Raheb, Mitri. "Christlich-islamischer Dialog in Palästina." *CIBEDO: Beiträge zum Gespräch zwischen Christen und Muslimen* 10 (1996) 8–11.

Bouwen, Frans. "Prier et vivre pour l'unité à Jérusalem à la lumière de l'encyclique 'Ut unum sint'. " *Proche*-Orient Chrétien 45 (1995) 132–42.

Deckwerth, Michae. "Versöhnung: Vom Ge- und Mißbrauch eines Wortes." Mission 1 (1995) 7–10.

Khoury, Geries Sa'ed. "Todistus, solidaarisus ja Kultuuri." *Ekumeeneien Vuosikira, Helsinki* (1995) 49–56.

Krupp, Michael. "Die Stimme eines christlichen Palästinensers." *EvTh* 55 (1995) 292–5.

Meinardus, Otto. "The Copts in Jerusalem and the Question of the Holy Places." *Coptic Church Review* 16 (1995) 9–25.

Raheb, Mitri. "Nabots Weinberg: eine Landrechtsfrage." *Darum: Zeitschrift des Evangelischen Missionswerkes in Südwestdeutschland e.V., für die Freunde des Missionswerkes* 1 (1995) 5.

Raheb, Mitri. "Olivenbäume der Hoffnung pflanzen: Der Friedensprozeß stellt die Christen Palästinas vor neue Aufgaben." *Der Überblick* 31:4 (1995) 39–42.

Raheb, Mitri. "Vom Wehgeschrei zum Freudengelaechter: Gott wird Mensch. Die gute Botschaft von Christi Geburt-im Kontext des Ringens und der Kaempfe in Palaestina."*Publik-Forum* 24:24 (1995) 6–8.

Raheb, Mitri. "Educational Co-operation among Christians, Muslims and Jews in the Middle East." *British Journal of Religious Education* 18:1 (1995) 59–62.

Raheb, Viola. "Maria und Elisabeth." *Schneller Magazin* 3 (1995).

Raheb, Viola. "Christen in Palästina." *Schritte* 5 (1995).

Rieger, Albert. "Theologie im Palästinensischen Kontext." *ZMiss* 21 (1995) 58–60.

Younan, Suad. "Koexistenz statt Konflikt: Versöhnung als Aufgabe von Juden, Christen und Muslimen." *Mission 1* (1995) 15–18.

Bishara, A. "The Arab Minority in Israel." *Theory and Criticism* 3 (1994) (in Hebrew).

Goetze, Andreas. "Kirche, Israel und die Palästinenser: Eine Nachlese zum Weltgebetstag der Frauen 1994." *Hessisches Pfarrerblatt* 3 (1994) 77–83.

Khoury, Geries Sa'ed. "La voix des prophètes." *Spiritus, Paris* 135 (1994) : 159–68.

Khoury, Rafiq. "L'insertion de nos Eglises dans le monde de l'islam arabe : Réflexion pastorales." *Documentation Catholique* 2087 (1994) : 140–43.

Peled, A., "The Crystallization of an Israeli Policy Towards Muslim and Christian Holy Places, 1948–1955", *The Muslim World* 84 (1994) 95–121.

Suermann, Harald. "Palästinensische Theologie im Zeitalter der Intifada." *Oriens Christianus* 78 (1994) 104–122.

Raheb, Viola. "Einander Hören und um Erlösung beten für alle." *Frauen Unterwegs: Zeitschrift der Evangelischen Frauenhilfe in Deutschland e.V.* 2 (1994).

Bechmann, Ulrike. "Gespür für die Leidenden." *Junge Kirche* 54 (1993) 663–70.

Bowman, Glenn. "Nationalizing the Sacred: Shrines and Shifting Identities in the Israeli-Occupied Territories." *Man: The Journal of the Royal Anthropological Institute* 28:3 (1993) 431–60.

Blewett, Tim. "Bible, Land, Justice—The Challenge of Na'im Ateek and Palestinian Theology." *Theology* 96:771 (1993) 209–16.

Hoffmann, Paul E. "Christen setzen auf Dialog: Bemühen um Objektivität im Konflikt zwischen Palästinensern und Israelis." *Mission* 2 (1993) 17–20.

Khoury, Rafiq. "Die arabisch-christliche Minderheit in Palästina." *DPG Info-Brief* 22 (1993), 23.

Mazawi, André Elias. "Palestinian Local Theology and the Issue of Islamo-Christian Dialogue: An Appraisal." *Islamochristiana* 19 (1993) 93–115.

Poley, Alexei. "Jérusalem des Coptes : Deux mille ans dans la ville sainte." *Le Monde Copte* 23 (1993) 49–57.

Raheb, Viola. "Mit Marthas und Maria Kräften." *Schneller Magazin* 4 (1993).

Tsimhoni, Daphne. "בעיית הזהות הלאומית של הערבים הנוצרים בירושלים ובגדה המערבית" ("The Problem of National Identity among Arab Christians in Jerusalem and the West Bank")" עיונים בתקומת ישראל; מאסף לבעיות הציונות, היישוב ומדינת ישראל. שדה בוקר (*Iyunim Bitkumat Israel*) 3 (1993) 469–96.

Tsimhoni, Daphne. "הפטריארכיה הלטינית של ירושלים ממחצית המאה ה-19 ועד ימינו: היבטים מוסדיים וחברתיים" ("The Latin [Roman Catholic] Patriarchate of Jerusalem from the Second Half of the Nineteenth Century till Today: Institutional and Social Aspects"). *Ha-Mizrah He-Hadash* 14 (1993) 115–38.

Watzal, Ludwig. "Notwendige Bemühungen mit bescheidenem Erfolg. Der Dialog zwischen den Religionen in Israel." *Herder-Korrespondenz* 47 (1993) 140–44.

Bräuer, Martin. "Kontextuelle Theologie in Palästina." *MdKI* 6 (1992) 113–15.

Gloel, Hans-Martin. "Palästinensische Befreiungstheologie, Arabische Christen suchen einen Weg zum Frieden." *Nachrichten der ev.-luth. Kirche in Bayern* 15/16 (1992) 294–6.

Kassab, Najla. "A Middle Eastern Christian Approach to the Old Testament." *ThRev* 1:13 (1992) 35–48.

Khodr, Georges. "العهد القديم والايمان المسيحي." *ThRev* 1:13 (1992) 49–58.

Kreutz, Andrej. "The Vatican and the Palestinians: A historical overview." *Islamochristiana* 18 (1992) 109–25.

Pleins, David J. "Is a Palestinian Theology of Liberation Possible?" *Anglican Theological Review* 74:2 (1992) 133–43.

Raheb, Viola. "Wir finden unseren eigenen Weg." *Schneller Magazin* 2 (1992).

Raheb, Viola. "Gemeinsam gehen- mit Marthas und Marias Kräften." *Frauen Unterwegs: Zeitschrift der Evangelischen Frauenhilfe in Deutschland e.V.* 8 (1992).

Wright, Lewis. "Anglicanism in the Holy Land; St George's Cathedral, Jerusalem." *Anglican and Episcopal History* 61:3 (1992) 379–82.

Lowe, Malcom. "Palästinensische Theologie: Vertreter, Ziele, Gefahren." *Nordelbische Stimmen* 1 (1991) 8–12.

Palmer, Andrew. "The History of the Syrian Orthodox in Jerusalem." *Oriens Christianus* 75 (1991)
10–24.

Sabella, Bernard and A. Pacini. "The Emigration of the Arab Christians: Dimensions and Causes of the Exodus." *Proche-Orient Chrétien* 47 (1991) 141–69.

Sabella, Bernard. "Palestinian Christian Emigration from the Holy Land." *Proche-Orient Chrétien* 41 (1991) 74–85.

Arens, Edmund. "Der schwierige Weg zur Solidarität: Theologische Beiträge zum Nahostkonflikt." *Orientierung* 3 (1990) 29–32.

Ateek, Naim. "Ein Friedenstraum: Vision eines Palästinensers." *Reformatio: Zeitschrift für Kultur, Politik, Kirche* 9 (1990) 419–24.

Bowman, Glenn. "Religion and Political Identity in Beit Sahour." *Middle East Report* 20:3–4 (1990) 50–53.

Chacour, Elias. "Is there Hope for Peace in the Middle East?" *Church and Society* 81 (1990) 67–76.

Khodr, Georges. "علامات على طريق الوحدة." ("Signs on the Road to Unity"). *ThRev* 1:11 (1990) 58–63.

Levinson, Nathan Peter. "Die Intifada und die Berliner Mission: Evangelische Akeademien woollen die aggressive 'palästinensische Theologie' verbreiten." *Allgemeine Jüdische Wochenzeitung* 38 (1990).

Levinson, Pnina Navè. "Kommt die Zeit der Erlösung durch die glorreiche Intifada? Die Gruppe 'Christen für Frieden im Heiligen Land' startet weltweite 'Gebetsoffensive' für die Palästinenser." *Allgemeine Jüdische Wochenzeitung* 12 (1990).

Lowe, Malcom. "Was ist palästinensiche Theologie?" *Die Zukunft* 3 (1990) 17.

Nassar, Naim. "Arab Christians an 'Endangered Species' of the West Bank" *MECC (Middle East Council of Churches) Perspectives* 8 (1990) 41–2.

Renard, John. "Theological Perspectives on the Middle East." *American-Arab Affairs* 34 (1990) 56–63.

Younan, Munib. "Reflections of a Palestinian Pastor." *Dialogue* 29 (1990) 33–6.

Ateek, Naim Sifan. "An Arab-Israeli's theological reflections on the state of Israel after 40 years." *Immanuel* 22/23 (1989) 102–19.

Daubenberger, Theo. "Preis der Hoffnung: Christen in der Intifada." *EPD-Entwicklungspolitik* 15 (1989) 32. Originally in *Die Weltmission* 2 (1989).

Hoffmann, Paul E. "Suche Frieden und jage ihm nach! Überlegungen zum evangelischen Engagement in der Diskussion um Frieden zwischen Israel und Palästina." *EPD-Entwicklungspolitik* 15 (1989) 27. Orginially in *Mission* 2 (1989) 18–23.

Matar, Nabil I. "Protestantism, Palestine, and Partisan Scholarship." *Journal of Palestine Studies* 18:4 (1989) 52–70.

Raheb, Mitri. "Christentum in zwei Welten: zum Thema Judenchristen und palästinensische Christen." *EPD-Entwicklungspolitik* 15 (1989) 21.

Raheb, Mitri. "Evangelische Theologie und Palaestina: Eine kritische Auseinandersetzung mit der deutschen 'Israel-Theologie.'" *EPD-Entwicklungspolitik* 15 (1989) 14–18.

Tsimhoni, Daphne. "The Political Configuration of the Christians in the State of Israel." *Hamizrah Hahadash* 32 (1989) 139–74 (in Hebrew).

Chacour, Elias. "On the Face of our Enemies: The Sermon on the Mount." *Plough* 20 (1988) 5–8.

Khoury, Rafiq. "Chrétiens arabes de la Terre sainte." *Etudes* 369:4 (1988) 395–408.

Ruether, Rosemary Radford. "Zionism and the Ideological Manipulation of Christian Groups." *American-Arab Affairs* 22 (1987).

Sapir, Sha'ul. "'הבישוף בליית ומפעלו בירושלים: קולג' סט. ג'ורג'" ("Bishop Blyth and his Jerusalem Legacy: St George's College"). קתדרה *(Cathedra)* 46 (1987) 45–64.

Yaffe, Aharon. "75") "הבפטיסטים בארץ הקדש: 75 שנות פעילות בפטיסתית בארץ־ישראל Years of Baptist Activities in Israel") 77–51 (1987) 20 אופקים בגיאוגרפיה.

Ateek, Naim. "Hope in a Hopeless World." *Evangelical Review of Theology* 10 (1986) 33–8.

Bowman, Glenn. "Unholy struggle on holy ground: conflict and its interpretation." *Anthropology Today* II (1986) 4–7.

Tsimhoni, Daphne. "Continuity and Change in Communal Autonomy: The Christian Communal Organisations in Jerusalem 1948–80." *Middle Eastern Studies* 22 (1986) 398–417.

Ateek, Naim. "Three Bible Meditations: Hope in a Hopeless World," *Theological Review* 1:6 (1985) 47–57.

Kafeety, Samir. "Message of Bishop Samir Kafeety, Met. of Jerusalem & the Middle East to the Episcopal Church." *Al Montada* 114–5 (1985) 30.

Tsimhoni, Daphne. "The Armenians and the Syrians: Ethno-Religious Communities in Jerusalem." *Middle Eastern Studies* 20:3 (1984) 352–69.

Tsimhoni, Daphne. "Between the Hammer and the Anvil: The National Dilemma of the Christian Minority in Jerusalem and the West Bank." *Orient* 24 (1983) 637–44.

Tsimhoni, Daphne. "Demographic Trends of the Christian Population in Jerusalem and the West Bank 1948–1978." *The Middle East Journal* 37 (1983) 54–63.

Tsimhoni, Daphne. "The Anglican (Evangelical Episcopal) Community in Jerusalem and the West Bank." *Oriente Moderno* (1983) 251–8.

Stöhr, Martin. "Warum das Verhältnis Kirche und jüdisches Volk nicht nur eine weiße, europäische Problematik ist." *ÖR* 1 (1982) 16–31.

Tsimhoni, Daphne. "The Greek Orthodox Community in Jerusalem and the West Bank, 1948–1978: A Profile of a Religious Minority in a National State." *Orient* 23:2 (1982) 281–98.

Zander, W. "Jurisdiction and Holiness: Reflections on the Coptic-Ethiopian Case." *Israel Law Review* 17 (1982).

Danilov, Stavro. "Dilemmas of Jerusalem's Christians." *Middle East Review* 13 (1981).

Tsimhoni, Daphne. "The Christian Communities in Jerusalem and the West Bank, 1948–1967." *Middle East Review* 9 (1976) 41–6.

Chacour, Elias. "The Attitude of a Christian Arab Twoards Israel." *Immanuel* 3 (1973–1974) 77–79.

Zander, Walter. "On the Settlement of Disputes about the Christian Holy Places." *Israel Law Review* 8:3 (1973) 331–66.

Khodr, Georges. "Theological Reflections of Eastern Christians on the Palestinian Problem." *Al Montada* 55 (1972) 18–23.

Löffler, Paul. "Theologians meet on Palestine. Report of a Consultation organized by NEEBII." *Al Montada* 55 (1972) 5–7.

Khodr, Georges. "World Conference of Christians for Palestine: Testimony of Bishop George Khodr." *Al Montada* 38–39 (1970) 21–2.

Löffler, Paul. "Analysis of the Ecumenical Situation of the Middle East from a Protestant Perspective." *Al Montada* 38–9 (1970) 23–30.

Schiloh, I.S. "Marriage and Divorce in Israel." *Israel Law Review* 5 (1970).

Stern, Gabriel. "Chronicles of the Armenian Orthodox Patriarchate of Jerusalem." *Christian News from Israel* 21:3 (1970) 6–8.

Kapeliouk, A. "L'État social, économique, culturel et juridique des Arabes chrétiennes en Israel." *Asian and African Studies* 5 (1969) 51–95.

Ajamian, S. "Brief Notes on the Armenian People and the Armenian Patriarchate of Jerusalem." *Christian News from Israel* 18 (1967) 37–48.

Khodr, Georges. "Palestine Between Biblical Texts and War." *Al Montada* 5–6 (1967) 8–9.

Meinardus, Otto. "The Nestorians in Egypt. A Note on the Nestorians in Jerusalem." *Oriens Christianus* 51 (1967) 112–29.

Meinardus, Otto. "Anachorétes modernes en Palestine." *Revue Biblique* 73 (1966) 119–27.

Salem, Gabriel. "The Monastery of S. Saba, and the Return of the Relics." *Eastern Churches Review* 1:1 (1966) 41–46.

Meinardus, Otto. "The Ethiopians in Jerusalem." *Zeitschrift für Kirchengeschichte* 76 (1965) 112–47, 217–32.

Meinardus, Otto. "The Syrian Jacobites in the Holy City." *Orientalia Suecana* 12 (1963) 60–82.

Wachtel, A., "The Church of the Nazarene in Israel", *Christian News from Israel* 11:4 (1960) 23.

Probst, B. "Das 'Swedish Theological Institute' in Jerusalem." *Judaica* 15:1 (1959) 62–4.

Downey, Glanville. "The Christian Schools of Palestine: A Chapter in Literary History." *Harvard Library Bulletin* 12 (1958) 297–319.

Mamour, Joseph. "Au Patriarcat Arménien de Jérusalem." *Proche-Orient Chrétien* 7 (1957) 65–69.

ARTICLES IN ENCYCLOPAEDIAS OR DICTIONARIES

Stephanous, Andera Zaki. "Middle Eastern and Arab Theology." Pages 537–41 in *Global Dictionary of Theology: A Resource for the Worldwide Church*. Edited by A. Dyrness and Veli-Matti Kärkkäinen. Downers Grove, IL: InverVarstiy, 2008.

Neuhaus, David M. "Palestinian liberation theology." Pages 328–9 in *A Dictionary of Jewish-Christian Relations*. Edited by Edward Kessler and Neil Wenborn. Cambridge: Cambridge University Press, 2005.

Stransky, Tom. "Tantur Ecumenical Institute." Page 970 in *Dictionary of the Ecumenical Movement*. Edited by Nicolas Lossky, José Míguez Bonino, and John Pobee. 2d ed.; Geneva, Switzerland: World Councel of Churches, 2002.

Sabella, Bernard. "Religious and Ethnic Minorities." Pages 346–9 in *Encyclopedia of the Palestinians*. Edited by Philip Mattar. New York: Facts on File, 2000.

UNPUBLISHED DISSERTATIONS AND THESES

Nylander, Marcus, "Liberating Liturgy: Liberation Theology Traits in Anglican and Lutheran Worship Services in Jerusalem and the West Bank." M.Th. Degree Essay, University of Lund, 2012.

Haiduc-Dale, Noah, and Zachary Lockman. "Nationalism and Religious Identification: Palestinian Christians in Mandate Palestine, 1918–1948." PhD diss., New York University, 2010.

Kuruvilla, Samuel Jacob. "Radical Christianity in the Holy Land: A Comparative Study of Liberation and Contextual Theology in Palestine-Israel." PhD diss., University of Exeter, 2009.

Bawalsa, Nadim Yousef, "Palestinian Christians: Emigration, the Occupation, and Political Islam." PhD dissertation, College of William and Mary, 2007.

Rishmawi, Saliba Hanna Saliba. "A Research Study Report on the Influence of Arab Christian Emigration on the Churches and its Holistic Ministry in the Bethlehem Region of The Holy Land." MA Thesis, Wartburg Theological Seminary, 2007.

Housten, Judy. "Towards Interdependence, Remembrance and Justice: Reconciliation Ministry in the Israeli/Palestinian Context." MA diss., All Nations Christian College, 2006.

Katanacho, Yohanna. "Investigating the Purposeful Placement of Psalm 86." PhD diss., Trinity International University, 2006.

Carlson, Leif. "Non-Violent action versus temptation to leave the Holy land: a Palestinian Christian perspective." MA thesis, Earlham School of Religion, 2005.

Castellan, Megan Laura. "From Nationalism to Liberation: The Palestinian Christians." PhD diss., College of William and Mary, 2005.

Hammon, Constance A. "Salaam-Shalom-Peace: A Fragmented Offering of Hope: Looking at Israel-Palestine through the Lens of Liberation Theology." D. Min thesis, San Francisco Theological Seminary, 2005.

Greenham, Anthony Bryan. "Muslim conversions to Christ: an investigation of Palestinian converts living in the Holy land." PhD diss., Southeastern Baptist Theological Seminary, 2004.

Lende, Gina. "A Quest for Justice: Palestinian Christians and their Palestinian Contextual Theology (1992–2002)." MA Thesis, University of Oslo, 2003.

Basha, Sami Saleem. "Contributions and involvements of the Christian Palestinian community in the educational work." Doctoral thesis, No. 513. PhD diss., Salesian Pontifical University, 2002.

Massad, Hanna. "The Theological Foundation for Reconciliation Between the Palestinian Christians and the Messianic Jews." PhD diss., Fuller Theological Seminary, 2000.

Carillet, Joel Andrew. "The Palestinian Church: An Ancient Body and Its Modern Challenges." Theological Research Exchange Network (Series) 062–0119.Thesis (MAR.), Emmanuel School of Religion, 1999.

Bechmann, Ulrike. "Vom Dialog zur Solidarität: Der christlich-islamische Dialog in Palästina am Beispiel des al-Liqâ'-Zentrums in Bethlehem." MA Thesis, Otto-Friedrich-Universität, Bamberg, 1996.

Schmidgal, Paul. "American Holiness Churches in the Holy Land, 1890–1994, Mission to Jews, Arabs and Armenians." PhD diss., Hebrew University of Jerusalem, 1996.

Peterson, Paul C. R. "The church's ministry of reconciliation in the Holy Land." D. Min. thesis, Fuller Theological Seminary, 1992.

Khoury, Rafiq. "La catéchèse dans l'Eglise locale de Jérusalem : Histoire, situation actuelle et perspectives d'avenir." PhD diss., Pontificia Universitas Lateranensis, Rome, 1978.

Kassees, A.S. "The People of Ramallah: A People of Christian Arab Heritage." PhD diss., Florida State University, 1970.

Betts, Robert Brenton. "The indigenous Arabic-speaking Christian communities of greater Syria and Mesopotamia : a history of their rites, a demographic survey of their geographical distribution and an analysis of their role in the political, social, and economic life of Lebanon, Syria, Jordan, Israel, and Iraq since national independence." PhD diss., Johns Hopkins University, 1968.

Kapeliouk, A. "Les Arabes chrétiens en Israel (1948–1967)." PhD diss., L'université de Paris, Sorbonne, 1968.

JOURNALS

مجلة اللقاء [Al-Liqa': Religious, Cultural & Social Magazine. A quarterly review (Jerusalem, since 1985)].

Al Liqa' Journal: A Bi-annual Palestinian Review Dedicated to the Study of Christianity, Islam, Christian-Jewish relations, Interfaith Dialogue in the Palestinian Context and to Cultural, Historical, Political, and Social issues (Jerusalem, since 1992).

Bulletin Diocésain du Patriarcat Latin de Jérusalem (Jerusalem).

Cornerstone: A Publication by Sabeel Ecumenical Liberation Theology Center (Jerusalem).

Im Lande der Bibel: Zeitschrift zur Information über evangelische Arbeit im Nahen Osten für die Mitglieder des Jerusalemvereins und Freunde und Förderer der Arbeit.

Mary's Well Occasional Papers (Online, out of Nazareth).

Religionen in Israel. Vierteljahresschrift über die Arbeit der Gesellschaft für Interreligiöse Verständigung in Israel sowie über Religion, Ökumene, Archäologie, Menschenrechte, Kultur und das Zusammenleben von Juden, Christen und Moslems in Israel, in der palästinensischen Autonomie und in den besetzten Gebieten. Herausgegeben von der Gesellschaft für Interreligiöse Verständigung in Israel (Israel Interfaith Association—IIA) (Jerusalem, since 1995).

Bibliography

Aburish, Said. *Arafat: From Defender to Dictator*. New York: Bloomsbury, 1998.

Ahmed An-Na'im, Abdullahi. "The Islamic Law of Apostasy and its Modern Applicability: A Case from the Sudan." *Religion* 16 (1986) 197–224.

Ajaj, Azar. "Baptism and the Muslim Convert to Christianity." *St Francis Magazine* 6/4 (2010) 595–611.

Ammerman, Nancy. "Religious Identities and Religious Institutions." In *Handbook of the Sociology of Religion*, edited by Michele Dillon, 207–44. Cambridge: Cambridge University Press, 2003.

Association of Baptist Churches. "The Nazareth Centre for Christian Studies." *Global Missiology* 4/2 (2007) n.p. http://ojs.globalmissiology.org/index.php/english/article/view/69/204.

Ateek, Naim Stifan. *Justice and Only Justice: A Palestinian Theology of Liberation*. Maryknoll, NY: Orbis, 1989.

Beit-Hallahmi, Benjamin. *Prologomena to the Psychological Study of Religion*. London: Associated University Press, 1989.

Bowman, Glenn. "Nationalizing and De-Nationalizing the Sacred: Shrines and Shifting Identities in the Israeli-Occupied Territories." In *Sacred Space in Israel and Palestine: Religion and Politics*, edited by Marshall J. Breger, Yitzhak Reiter, and Leonard Hammer, 195–227. London: Routledge, 2012.

Chacour, Elias. *Blood Brothers: The Dramatic Story of a Palestinian Christian Working for Peace in Israel*. 2nd and enl. ed. Grand Rapids: Chosen, 2003.

Coe, Shoki. "In Search of Renewal in Theological Education." *Theological Education* 9/4 (1973) 233–43.

———. "Theological Education—A Worldwide Perspective." *Theological Education* 11/1 (1974) 5–12.

Colbi, Saul P. *The Growth and Development of Christian Church Institutions in the State of Israel*. Jerusalem: Israel Economist, 1972.

———. *A Short History of Christianity in the Holy Land*. Jerusalem: Am Hassefer, 1965.

Douglas, Mary. *Purity and Danger: An Analysis of Concepts of Pollution and Taboo*. New York: Praeger, 1966.

"Dr. Dwight Baker." *Al Kalima* 1 (2007) 12.

Dumper, Michael. "Faith and Statecraft: Church-State Relations in Jerusalem after 1948." In *Palestinian Christians: Religion, Politics and Society in the Holy Land*, edited by A. O'Mahony, 9–55. London: Melisende, 1999.

Ehrlich, Avrum. "The Developing Attitudes of Arab Christianity towards the State of Israel." *Parole de l'Orient* 30 (2005) 481–531.

El-Assal, Riah Abu. *Caught in Between: The Story of an Arab Palestinian Christian Israeli.* London: SPCK, 1999.

Emmett, Chad F. *Beyond the Basilica: Christians and Muslims in Nazareth.* University of Chicago Geography Research Paper 237. Chicago: University of Chicago Press, 1995.

Farah, Fuad D. *Christian Presence in the Holy Land.* Nazareth: Fuad Farah, 2011.

Gaudeul, Jean-Marie. *Called from Islam to Christ: Why Muslims Become Christians.* East Sussex: Monarch, 1999.

Gavlak, Dale. "Evangelical Collective: New Association Seeks More Rights in Israel." *Christianity Today* 49/6 (May 2005) n.p. http://www.christianitytoday.com/ct/2005/june/9.24.html.

Gräbe, Uwe. *Kontextuelle palästinensische Theologie: Streitbare und umstrittene Beiträge zum ökumenischen und interreligiösen Gespräch.* Missionswissenschaftliche Forschungen. New Series 9. Erlangen: Erlanger Verlag für Mission und Ökumene, 1999.

Green, Tim. "Identity Issues for Ex-Muslim Christians, with Particular Reference to Marriage." *St Francis Magazine* 8/4 (2012) 435–81.

Greenham, Anthony. "A Study of Palestinian Muslim Conversions to Christ." *St Francis Magazine* 6/1 (February 2010) 116–75.

Hill, Phil. "Do Jesus and Paul Agree with the OT Laws Concerning Marriage, Divorce, and Remarriage?" *Mary's Well Occasional Papers* 1/5 (2012) 1–26.

Horenczyk, G., and S. J. Munayer. "Acculturation Orientations Toward Two Majority Groups: The Case of Palestinian Arab Christian Adolescents in Israel." *Journal of Cross-Cultural Psychology* 38/1 (2007) 76–86.

Ireland, Michael. "Israeli Baptist Seek to Raise Money for Ministry Center in Nazareth." *ASSIST News Service*, 2003. http://www.assistnews.net/Stories/2003/s03100149.htm.

Jørgensen, Jonas Adelin. *Jesus Imandars and Christ Bhaktas: Two Case Studies of Interreligious Hermeneutics and Identity in Global Christianity.* Frankfurt am Main: Peter Lang, 2008.

Kaartveit, Baard Helge. "The Christians of Palestine: Strength, Vulnerability, and Self-Restraint within a Multi-Sectarian Community." *Middle Eastern Studies* 49/5 (2013) 732–49.

Katanacho, Yohanna. *The Land of Christ: A Palestinian Cry.* Bethlehem: Bethlehem Bible College, 2012. Repr., Eugene, OR: Pickwick, 2013.

Kraft, Kathryn Ann. *Searching for Heaven in the Real World: A Sociological Discussion of Conversion in the Arab World.* New York: Regnum, 2013.

Kuruvilla, Samuel J. *Radical Christianity in Palestine and Israel: Liberation and Theology in the Middle East.* Library of Modern Religion 19. London: Tauris Academic Studies, 2012.

Lis, Jonathan. "Netanyahu Announces New Forum to Encourage Christian Arabs to Serve in Military." *Haaretz,* August 6, 2013. http://www.haaretz.com/news/national/.premium-1.539957.

Lowe, Malcolm. "Who Are the Heads of Churches in Jerusalem?" Gatestone Institute, January 29, 2014. http://www.gatestoneinstitute.org/4142/jerusalem-churches.

Lybarger, Loren D. "For Church or Nation? Islamism, Secular-Nationalism, and the Transformation of Christian Identities in Palestine." *Journal of the American Academy of Religion* 75/4 (2007) 777–813.

Mack, Merav. "Christian Palestinian Communities in Israel: Tensions Between Laity, Clergy, and State." In *Sacred Space in Israel and Palestine: Religion and Politics*, edited by Marshall J. Breger, Yitzhak Reiter, and Leonard Hammer, 284–310. London: Routledge, 2012.

Mansour, Ahmed Subhy. *The Penalty of Apostasy*. Toronto: International, 1998.

Mansour, Atallah. *Narrow Gate Churches: The Christian Presence in the Holy Land under Muslim and Jewish Rule*. Pasadena, CA: Hope, 2004.

Mansour, Bader. "A Brief Summary of Baptist History in the Holy Land: 1911–2011." 2012. http://baptist.org.il/baptistdata/en-events/d/0/0/ev107/files/100-Years-of-Baptist-Witness-in-the-Holy-Land.pdf.

———. "The Nazareth Center for Christian Studies." *Global Missiology English* 2 (2007) n.p. http://ojs.globalmissiology.org/index.php/english/article/view/69/204.

McGahern, Una. *Palestinian Christians in Israel: State Attitudes Towards Non-Muslims in a Jewish State*. Durham Modern Middle East and Islamic World 22. London: Routledge, 2011.

Miller, Duane Alexander. "Living among the Breakage: Contextual Theology-Making and Ex-Muslim Christians." PhD diss., University of Edinburgh, 2014.

———. "Renegotiating the Boundaries of Evangelicalism in Jerusalem's Christian Quarter." *Anglican and Episcopal History* 79/2 (2010) 185–88.

Moon, Ruth. "Christians Fight Israel's Marriage Ban." *Christianity Today* 56/10 (2012) n.p. http://www.christianitytoday.com/ct/2012/november/marriage-petition.html.

Morris, Benny. *The Birth of the Palestinian Refugee Problem Revisited*. Cambridge: Cambridge University Press, 2004.

Nerel, Gershon. *Anti-Zionism in the "Electronic Church" of Palestinian Christianity*. Analysis of Current Trends in Antisemitism 27. Jerusalem: SICSA, 2006.

O'Mahony, Anthony. "Palestinian Christians: Religion, Politics, and Society, c. 1800–1948." In *Palestinian Christians: Religion, Politics and Society in the Holy Land*, edited by A. O'Mahony, 9–55. London: Melisende, 1999.

Prittie, Terence. *Whose Jerusalem?* London: Frederick Muller, 1981.

Ramon, Amnon. "The Christian Institutions and the Fence around Jerusalem." In *The Security Fence around Jerusalem: Implications for the City and its Residents*, edited by Israel Kimhi, 119–136. Jerusalem: The Jerusalem Institute for Israel Studies, 2006.

———. נצרות ונוצרים במדינת היהודים: המדיניות הישראלית הכנסיות והקהילות הנוצריות *(1948–2010)*. [*Christians and Christianity in the Jewish State: Israeli Policy towards the Churches and the Christian Communities (1948–2010)*]. The JIIS Studies 420. Jerusalem: The Jerusalem Institute for Israel Studies, 2012.

Reynolds, Jeremy. "Baptists in Israel Celebrate 100 Years of Ministry." *ASSIST News* (2012). http://www.assistnews.net/Stories/2011/s11040134.htm.

Sabella, Bernard. "Socio-economic Characteristics and Challenges to Palestinian Christians in the Holy Land." In *Palestinian Christians: Religion, Politics and Society in the Holy Land*, edited by A. O'Mahony, 82–95. London: Melisende, 1999.

Schmid, Muriel. "From the Church of the Nativity to the Churches of the World: Palestinian Christians and Their 'Cry of Hope.'" *Theology Today* 69/4 (2013) 428–40.

Stanley, Brian. "Inculturation: Historical Background, Theological Foundations and Contemporary Questions." *Transformation* 24/1 (2007) 21–27

Syrjänen, Seppo. *In Search of Meaning and Identity: Conversion to Christianity In Pakistani Muslim Culture*. Helsinki: Finnish Society for Missiology and Ecumenics, 1984.

Tsimhoni, Daphne. *Christian Communities in Jerusalem and the West Bank since 1948: An Historical, Social and Political Study*. Westport, CT: Praeger, 1993.

———. "Palestinian Christians and the Peace Process: The Dilemma of a Minority." In *The Middle East Peace Process: Interdisciplinary Perspectives*, edited by Ilan Peleg, 141–60. New York: State University of New York, 1998.

Watts, Mrs. James W. *Palestinian Tapestries*. Richmond: Foreign Mission Board of the Southern Baptist Convention, 1936.

Weiner, Justus Reid. *Human Rights of Christians In Palestinian Society*. Jerusalem: Jerusalem Center for Public Affairs, 2005. http://www.jcpa.org/text/Christian-Persecution-Weiner.pdf.

Woodberry, J. Dudley, Russell G. Shubin, and G. Marks. "Why Muslims Follow Jesus." *Christianity Today* (October, 2007) n.p. www.christianitytoday.com/ct/2007/october/42.80.html.

Yaffe, Aharon. "הבפטיסטים בארץ הקדש: 75 שנות פעילות בפטיסתית בארץ־ישראל" ["75 Years of Baptist Activities in Israel"]. אופקים בגיאוגרפיה 20 (1987) 51–77.

Yousef, Mossab Hassan. *Son of Hamas: A Gripping Account of Terror, Betrayal, Political Intrigue, and Unthinkable Choices*. Carol Stream, IL: SaltRiver, 2010.

Lightning Source UK Ltd.
Milton Keynes UK
UKOW06f0146060816

280074UK00002B/53/P